That's why they call it
WORK
Because it isn't easy

BOOK THREE OF THE TRILOGY BY
WILLIAM A. GRALNICK

For information regarding permission, please write to: info@barringerpublishing.com

Barringer Publishing, Naples, Florida
www.barringerpublishing.com

Cover and layout by Linda S. Duider

ISBN: #978-1-954396-55-5

Library of Congress Cataloging-in-Publication Data
That's Why They Call It Work

Printed in U.S.A.

To my special angel, who becomes more special every day.

CONTENTS

ACKNOWLEDGEMENTS

*To my readers, Stuart Silver and Paul
("remove that comma") Horowitz, a lifetime
supply of eye drops and eternal thanks.*

*A salute to Jeffrey Thol who spent one
and a half hours on the cover shot.*

*Heartfelt thanks for a true hero, Gen. Uri Bar-Lev
who trusted me even with his name.*

PREFACE

When the New York School District stopped the teaching of sentence diagramming, she had a conniption fit.

The writing seed got planted in my brain when I realized my mother was dead serious, shutting me out of an adult conversation with this: "Little pishers (Yiddish for pee-ers or pissers) should be seen and not heard."

Then, too, my older brother was a high school journalist. That bud was about to flower into a career of national recognition as a television news producer, executive producer, and several vice presidencies of network news divisions. He was always writing.

The Midwood High School award-winning newspaper was *The Argus*. Miss Marion Mulhern was the school's journalism teacher and faculty head of *The Argus*. She had white hair on her head and her chinny-chin-chin. She wore "space shoes." Popular in the '50s, space shoes were custom-made walking cushions for people with bad feet. Clompy? Clumpy? For sure ugly. But she could teach, and she saw

Midwood High School—a great high school at a great time.

talent. I chose not to follow my brother onto the paper. I wanted to be a jock. But I took her course, and it spoke to me.

Miss Ennis was my eighth-grade English teacher. Her hair was corn-colored, and she wore normal old lady shoes, black lace-ups with chock-a-block heels. A beast was what she was when it came to English. When the New York City School District decided to stop teaching sentence diagramming, she had a conniption fit. An enduring one. It was as if someone decided students would no longer be allowed to learn how to breathe, swallow, or eat lunch. As I sit here, more than 65 years from Miss Ennis, as a writer, I've learned she was right. Maybe a little screwy about it, but right, nonetheless.

The flint of love sparked my first explosion of writing. I had a serious relationship, or at least I thought it was, throughout three years of high school and a year of college. Came college, and I found out that only one of us was serious. She lived on Long Island, and I lived in Brooklyn. I therefore wrote to her since she was a long-distance phone call away that cost money, and a call having to be made while hemmed in by prying ears. I mean it when I tell you I wrote over 500 letters during that time.

I didn't know it then, but I suffered from depression. I think all humorists do. Charles Shultz's Charlie Brown spoke to my heart. Adding a touch of creativity, I'd paste a meaningful comic strip to the back of the envelope. The family's mail carrier gave her hell when she broke up with me. "Do you know how boring it is to deliver mail?" he chastised her. "That kid's letters made my day!" So, I had a fan—something for which writers live. Then came college English.

I don't remember the professor's name. I do remember he was a hateful man. He didn't believe in freshman creativity, and since I knew a spectacularly small amount about English grammar (proving Miss Ennis right), I got an F on my mid-term. That's when it all changed. I went home, tail between my legs, or maybe pen is the correct word, to humbly confess the truth to my brother. His response? He wasn't having any of it. I was to give up most of my Thanksgiving holiday plans and prepare to learn how to write. Not easy, but thanks to Miss

Ennis, Charlie Brown, and finally, my brother, my F went to a B. It was my lowest grade in making Dean's List the first semester.

Lincoln said, "Once the bug of politics has bitten you, you get a virus from which you're never cured." So, it is with writing. Once you've seen your byline in print, you develop a lifelong fever. Enter *Newsday Newspaper*, the major print voice of Long Island, New York.

I was mindlessly watching a mindless show in my Freeport, Long Island apartment. It was *The Adventures of Ozzie and Harriet Show*. Suddenly, I felt something going on in my head; this is often the case for me . . . I realized this show was mindless and that Ozzie and Harriet bore no semblance to reality or the reality I knew about my family and friends' families. I wrote a reasonably piquant critique, and low and behold. I was a published author in one of the most respected newspapers in the country. All at the age of 25—a budding Hemmingway I was. If you believe the Hemmingway part, I've got a bridge in Brooklyn . . . The icing on the cake? A large graphic topped the piece. The bug had bitten me. The virus had struck.

But I had to make a living. The $25.00 I got for the article would hardly buy groceries. Writing was out; work was in.

WILLIAM A. GRALNICK

"A blank piece of paper is God's way of telling us how hard it is to be God."

– Sidney Sheldon

"There are three rules for writing a novel. Unfortunately, no one knows what they are."

– W. Somerset Maugham
Bryn Donovan

Introduction

This book is comfort food in the form of words.

"An introduction introduces readers to the manuscript's main topics and prepares them for what they can expect," says the writer's manual. Here goes. This book is the third and final book of a memoir trilogy. It covers life as a working stiff. However, if I reach my goal, you won't find it stiff. While many don't see much funny or humorous about work, that could be because they aren't viewing it the right way. As shown in the first two books, my tap dance through life has put me in many an Alice in Wonderland moment. It's the same for work. You'll both scratch your head and smile.

In this book, you'll meet an almost adult who has graduated from graduate school and secures his first real job from an index card on a bulletin board. From there, you'll board a literary train chugging through six states and some key cities in them. You'll watch me through the window as I forge a path through them. Some of the stops are planned. Then again as Shaw wrote, ". . . the best laid plans of mice and men often go awry." The train ends up taking some unanticipated spur lines.

The book is designed to be light and easy to read. It is comfort food in the form of words. You should find reading it enjoyable.

"When I was a little boy, they called me a liar, but now that I am a grown-up they call me a writer."

– Isaac Bashevis Singer

You may tell a tale that takes up residence in someone's soul, becomes their blood and self and purpose. That tale will move them and drive them and who knows what they might do because of it, because of your words. That is your role, your gift.

– Erin Morgenstern,
The Night Circus

Book One

The Early Years

The grocery store, a place for everything.

Imagine pounding those keys—I'd give the food away first . . .

Water, Snow, and Perfume

I knew immediately I would need to make some money.

In high school, I got my first job. I was a stock boy at the neighborhood Bohack's. The top people wore white aprons. Sawdust covered the floor. The cash register was as big and heavy as a large boulder. It was like an old typewriter, but pounding the keys gave you numbers instead of letters. I hated it.

Then I discovered the Atlantic Beach Hotel on Atlantic Beach, Long Island. It was the summer before college. My parents told me I would get a $20-a-week "allowance" in college. I was on the food plan, so they reasoned I wouldn't need much money. I knew immediately I needed to make some money. There was more to do in college than eat and study. Someone told me there were hotels along the beach, some of which were "seasonal." People checked in on Memorial Day and checked out on Labor Day. You can find the details of that adventure in, *The War of the Itchy Balls and Other Tales from Brooklyn*. On Labor Day, I too, checked out. I had earned $1,200 in mostly twenty-five cent tips. Things for the freshman year were looking up.

Eventually, the quarters were gone, or the money I had turned them into was. I needed a steady job. This one, including my first adult theft, can be found in *George Washington Never Slept Here*. Also found in that book are stories about my days as a tourist guide in the District of Columbia. One of which points out that dropping dead in a cemetery, which one of my clients did, is a bad thing to do. At the end of my master's degree, I needed a real job, the hunt for which begins this book. Read on!

Coal mining: a job or a death sentence?

Pennsylvania

JOHNSTOWN

Next to every chair, there was a spittoon.

Don't spit on the floor, remember the Johnstown Flood.

●●●

The process of getting a job in the '60s was like the Jurassic Park era compared to now. Job notices posted on corkboards beckoned for attention. In the case of GW, thumbtacks affixed the offerings. I was trying to get out of a messy relationship in Washington, DC, so it mattered not to me where the job was, so long as it was far away from DC, challenging to get to, and preferably both. I found a post looking for someone acquainted with state and local government (that was my minor) and who was young. Most interestingly, it said, "Pipe smokers need not apply." I didn't smoke a pipe at that time

5

(I had a short fling with it in college) or anything else, so I applied. Home run. I got the job.

It certainly had an interest factor. The Greater Johnstown Committee was a non-profit that could be called a very big fish in a small pond. To be a member, one had to be the president of a company or the senior executive of one. For instance, one of the members was the CEO of Bethlehem Steel. He wasn't Bethlehem Steel's president, just of its works in this area—still a huge deal.

Johnstown was a steel and coal town. The committee's members included the heads of Bethlehem and U.S. Steel and a coal company. The president of the largest department store, the president of the Water Company, the senior executive of the Pennsylvania Electric Power Company, and so on were all on the board. Each year the committee did an analytical report on Johnstown's needs. Most of it became the city council's agenda. I'll get to what we did. Step aside with me for a moment.

Once I became the father of adult children, I would occasionally listen to my sons complain about how hard college was. I would tell them it wouldn't be long before they realized, looking back, that this was the best part of life. Soon they did. Then they complained about how hard work was. My retort? "That's why they call it work." Hence the title.

An old political adage says that power corrupts, and absolute power corrupts absolutely. It would only be a year before I got to prove that but becoming an instant BMIT (Big Man In Town) was a hoot. For instance, Johnstown's Rotary invited me to be a member. Rotary was THE club in town and the one where my board members belonged. Everyone who was anyone wanted a word with me. I was treated like nitroglycerin, not because I might explode but because one of the people who supported me might.

Here's a hint of what the Johnstown of back then was like. Start with very conservative. It was Wallace Country then and now Trump country. It had unofficially segregated schools. Bussing was a topic that caused instant heat. A residential section above the town was monikered with the very un-PC name of Coon Ridge. Johnstown had dilapidated housing. The air quality was unhealthy and, for some, could be fatal. It was a tough town where shotguns and trucks were everywhere. My barber kept the shotgun next to his chair propped up in a corner, and his truck with the shotgun rack in front of the shop.

Another example. One of my officers invited me to lunch at the exclusive country club. He was the president of the local savings bank. He was known to snatch away overdue mortgages faster than clams snap shut. We were at the bar getting a drink when a very drunk member staggered up to us and said to my host, "When you die, I'm going to piss on your grave." Faster than that snapping clam shell, his retort, measured and cold as ice, was, "I hope you don't mind standing in line." Then he turned back to me, dismissing this guy without a moment's care. It was a learning experience in the exercise of power and, for me, learning how to deal with those who had power. I was not to be king, but I was running with the kingmakers. Machiavelli: "Better the kingmaker than the king." It took another lesson before I had it down pat.

Aside from an abundance of coal, Johnstown had plentiful water which, about 60 years before my arrival, had swept down a mountain creating the great Johnstown flood. Another notable fact was that Johnstown was also the seat of the Carpatho-Russian Church in America.

From the above several paragraphs, likely you are wondering, *What? Who? So what?* Here are the answers. We'll start with the pipe which for some reason I kept in a sweat sock. My predecessor, about twenty years older than me, had a Ph.D., and smoked a pipe. He was good at telling folks what to do but not much good at doing anything. Hence the "no pipe smokers need apply." The board decided that smoking a pipe and doing nothing were synonymous. In my interview, I told them I was interested in the doing. I wanted to take the piles of research that Mr. Pipe-Smoker had created and turn them into action. That got me the job.

And the church? My name is Russian, so they wrongly assumed I was Christian. You know what they say about assumptions. The

"So what?", is this. Johnstown's power elite was racist, anti-Semitic and the job they hired me for came with membership to a country club that didn't take Jews as members. Whoops. My chairman called on the first Sunday in town, very apologetic. They didn't think to ask about my church affiliation. "Tell me where you'd like to worship. I'll come to pick you up and get you there," he said. Then came the terrible truth, met with absolute silence on the other end of the phone. "Thank you, sir, but I'm Jewish."

Monday morning, at a quickly called meeting, they explained the facts of life in Johnstown, Pennsylvania. I had a choice. They could put my name up for membership but doubted that even they could get me accepted or they would give me in money what the first year's dues would have cost them. Of course, being young, idealist, Jewish, and from Brooklyn, I chose door number one. They kept their word. It cost me several thousand liberal dollars. They backed my application and paid for my membership in the Rotary Club. The soundest object lesson was yet to come.

School ended. In late fall, my master's degree still needed a finished thesis, but the university was kind enough to let me do it *in absentia* with specific obligations on my part. I drove from Washington, DC, to Johnstown. I've always been an observer. What did I observe? Strange piles of black (I had no idea what it was) stuff, some taller than houses. I saw men and women sitting on porches staring vacantly at nothing. A force of some kind seemed to press them into their rocking chairs. They looked old before their time, worn, dressed in tatters, and expressionless. As the sun set, I noticed red hues on the hillsides. What struck me most was the yellow dust that covered everything, the streets, trees, and cars. I thought it was pollen. It wasn't.

Once passed the formality of my membership in the Rotary Club, I was invited to give an address on *The Future of Johnstown*. "Into the Valley of Death, Rode the Six Hundred . . ." That wasn't the title of the talk. It was the result. I would be one of the riders but before the speech, I had some things I had to do in a hurry. One was to find a place to live. The first time in my young life I ever had to do this became another learning experience. I should have known from the address, 950½ Carnegie Avenue, that something would be different. It was an outside walk up to a quaint, small apartment that I was to discover, after I signed the lease, had no closets. Yes, you read it right. It had no closets, as in none. Fortunately, I didn't have a lot of clothing. I got creative and made do.

I had to set up my office and meet my secretary, Carol, who came with the office. I was dictating some letters; she was taking shorthand. We weren't in sync. Finally, she said, "Mr. Gralnick . . . (which shook me as she had at least a dozen years on me), I'll bring in a typewriter. You just talk, and I'll type." I was skeptical. I shouldn't have been. She typed over a hundred words a minute flawlessly.

There were board members to meet and politicians to meet, including Mayor K.O. Thompkins, who looked like a large shmoo and pronounced parmesan cheese this way: "Par-mee-zien" as in, "Kid, pass me the parmeezien, please." I had my first city council meeting to attend. There, I discovered two new to me eye-openers. One was a sign that said, for true, "Don't Spit on the Floor—Remember the Johnstown Flood." The other was that by the side of each chair, sat a spittoon. I guess that went with the warning about the flood.

KO was a character looking to become a bigger character. The election was coming up. He sold copy machines and probably didn't have enough customers to swing an election. He needed an issue. One day as the daily 100-car coal freight rumbled through downtown during rush hour, he had it. He wrote to the company demanding that the train not be run at that hour. He wanted it to be either before the morning rush hour or after the evening one. We must remember the size here. The train was big, but rush hour in Johnstown? Not so big. But KO threatened to block its passage before the entry to the city and hold it until rush hour was over. The railroad's response? He was told to mind his own business, that the city didn't own the tracks, the railroad did, that interfering with interstate commerce was a crime, and that he could get himself arrested if he didn't cool his jets. Now, the issue was big news.

Having been told to take a flying leap, KO decided to show them who was boss. He threw his hole card. The city's police cars sat on the tracks and stopped the rolling freight. Also rolling, if I remember correctly, were the railroad police and the state police. Faced with handcuffs, which would have been even bigger news, KO huffed and puffed, hung his head, and left. But he was re-elected, so his stunt worked.

Remember that Rotary invitation and my speech? Another lesson I'll never forget. This one was "know thy audience." Since my arrival, I had been ruminating about that yellow powder I'd seen while driving in. I'd already learned the black stuff was called "slag," the by-product of coal production. Amongst other things, it is toxic to the environment. And the yellow dust? Not pollen—a by-product of steel manufacturing. It was sulfur dioxide. It was ruinous to breathe over the long term. I also learned about another result of mining—black lung disease. The name tells it all. From poorly ventilated mines, miners breathed in deadly air whose black coal dust coated their lungs which looked black on x-rays. It caused either emphysema or cancer. Once you got it, it was a death sentence.

I crafted these ills into a "what a wonderful world it would be" kind of speech, indicating that with the right actions, Johnstown could become Brigadoon. Not! But it was an inspiring speech that brought cheers and applause from all the members who were not community leaders. That I hadn't noticed until much later. As if someone was timing me, about two seconds after I walked through my office door, Carol said, "Mr. George Hand said to come to his office—right now." She added, "Mr. Gralnick, he didn't sound very happy." And who was this Mr. Impatient? He was the PR Director at Bethlehem Steel, and, oh yes, his boss was an officer of the Greater Johnstown Committee. I thought he wanted to give me tips on my speech. Tips weren't exactly what were forthcoming.

Downtown Johnstown at that time was compact. It was maybe a ten-minute walk to see Mr. Hand. His secretary ushered me into his office. As I began to sit, he said, "Don't bother sitting; this won't take long." I saw the clouds rolling in. His tip on the speech? I shouldn't have given it, and I'd better not give one like it again.

They came like bullets from a machine gun—statistics about what Bethlehem means to the economy of the city and the region. It was impressive—if one didn't investigate the opposite side of the coin. He dressed me down, was little interested, no, totally not interested, in anything I might have to say for myself, and ended it with, "I want this to be the last time we have this chat." On the way out, a lot less steady than when I came in, I noticed a parking lot sign saying, "If you're not driving an American car, you can't park here." A none-too-subtle reminder that foreign cars didn't use Bethlehem's steel; therefore, buying one meant taking jobs from the men and women who were your neighbors and friends. Fortunately, I had walked. My car was a red VW Beetle.

Such were the first two weeks of my first job. I did grow into it. I discovered that the TV station and newspaper were often interested in what I had to say. I had learned what was supposed to be said, so I was safe when the interviews came. I would soon be doing op-eds for the paper. The job was devoid of a honeymoon period. I was thrown into the pool, but that was better than being thrown into a blasting furnace. My name was neither Meshack nor Abednego, but I survived and started work.

In two and a half years, here's a list of what the Greater Johnstown Committee accomplished under my pipeless leadership:

- Wrote a paper to the governor on why Johnstown should be the first city chosen in the governor's newly announced partnership-city program. With my board behind me, the state honored us, opening the spigots of state money for the city.
- Built numerous mini parks in depressed areas.
- Created a winter ski run on a hillside abandoned because of mining.
- Rehabilitated a military cemetery that was re-opened with a U.S. Air Force flyover, courtesy of soon-to-be, Congressman John P. Murtha, a genuine war hero.

- Built a parking garage for the congested downtown.
- Did the first inner-city housing study ever commissioned by the city council.
- Obtained funds for a nearby town where many retired, disabled miners, lived. The town used the money to turn the downtown's facades into their historic likenesses, so downtown didn't look like the miner's faces.
- Brought black and white leadership together after MLK's assassination, which had never happened, to discuss what to do to prevent in Johnstown the same race riot that was occurring in cities all over the country.

There was more. Speaking at meetings, driving to the state capitol in Harrisburg to meet the cabinet member in charge of the Partnership-City grab bag, and doing on-site research for the mini-park program and the housing study were all part of the job. And therein lies one heck of a tale.

Doing research in the library (remember, no Google), I found an article that gave Baltimore an A+ in the mini-park movement. I called the person noted as the principal cog in that machine and made an appointment to see him. There also was no cable news or satellite radio. On the way, I listened to music. Martin Luther King, Jr. had been assassinated, but I was oblivious to that fact. There were neither satellite-driven GPS nor cell phones to give directions. So, I also was clueless about Baltimore having exploded in a spontaneous riot. The governor had called out the National Guard, which was rolling into town along with me. Periodically slipping a look at my AAA trip-tik, I was startled when I looked up, and a flaming mattress flew off a roof landing about twenty yards in front of me. Startled, did I say? I slammed on the brakes and froze. A policeman came a-runnin'.

He assumed I was a troublemaker until he saw me—young, white, dressed in a suit, and clearly in the wrong place at the wrong time. He opened with, "What the hell are you doing here? Don't you know what's going on?" By then, I certainly knew something was going on. Army trucks bearing troops were rolling by. Anything not nailed down was flying off roofs. Molotov cocktails rained fire from the sky. People were smashing storefronts and carrying off anything they could lift. The cop filled me in on the rest and signaled to another cop, saying, "Get this jerk back to the highway before he gets killed." I had a lights and sirens motorcycle escort out of town. Don't tell anyone but . . . it was pretty cool.

At the two-year mark in Johnstown, a doctor who had become my mentor advised me to pack my bags. He said that people who stayed in Johnstown too long never left. The best they could do was be that big fish, but the pond would not get any bigger. He told me I had too much potential for that and that if I were smart, I'd leave to further my education and career. Both opportunities were to present themselves simultaneously.

Before leaving Johnstown, let's rejoin the discussion of power and influence. The state had plied Johnstown with hundreds of thousands of dollars. This resulted in the shaking of a coterie of hands, friendships shared, and business deals made. Once retired, the governor went into business. He hooked up with a group of investors betting that cable TV would revolutionize the world's viewing habits. They needed a test market. Johnstown owed him. It was an obvious choice.

Pre-council backroom meetings moved the process. The community heard the pitches made to the citizens' groups and the city council. Finally, came the vote on the various funds needed to put in cable. The Republicans were the council's majority. It was a party-line vote and passed. All was well. Everything was up to date in Johnstown, Pennsylvania. That is until investigators discovered that votes had been bought. I heard they went for $5,000 bucks per vote. Here's an example of how Johnstown's political machine was behind the times. At the same time, the mayor of Jersey City, Hugh Addonizio, was convicted by a jury of taking a bribe. His vote went for $100,000. Yes, the guys in Johnstown, who were arrested and jailed, were both crooks and chumps.

"Hard work never killed anybody, but why take a chance?"

– Edgar Bergen, famous ventriloquist, father of Charley McCarthy

The brain is a wonderful organ; it starts working the moment you get up in the morning and does not stop until you get into the office.

– Robert Frost, American poet

Colorado

BOULDER

He said, "You can't make good tasting beer with clean water."

Boulder in August is 80 degrees, 20% humidity, and snow on the mountain tops.

●●●

    I took my mentor's advice. I enrolled in the poly sci Ph.D. program at the University of Colorado and, through power company contacts, was recommended for the executive director's position at a new non-profit called, "Boulder Tomorrow." It offered half-time work. The chairman of the Political Science Department tendered me a teaching assistantship. I now had stitched together a livable income and, being a quick study, rented an apartment with several closets.

Here is a list of what the board of "Boulder Tomorrow" had for me to do:

- Nothing
- Nothing
- Nothing
- Nothing

In retrospect, that may have been the idea, to do a favor for the power boys in Johnstown, get me out of there, and safely tucked into something that would cause no trouble. I don't remember the office. I don't remember the secretary. The board members of the Greater Johnstown Committee are indelibly imprinted on my mind. Show me a picture lineup of the board members in Boulder, I couldn't point out one.

Boulder and Johnstown had one thing in common. They were both very conservative. Johnstown was "Wallace Country" when I was there. Boulder was a much more western, clean-cut, starched cowboy shirt open at the collar, or string tie with a slide on the tie, the slide that often matched the belt buckle on the jeans. Johnstown was rolling hills set off by the Appalachian Mountains that ran seven or eight thousand feet in height. Boulder was at the end of the Great Plains heading west and butted up against the Rocky Mountains, which often showed snow in August. I didn't much like either place. Johnstown had winter snow and ice. Boulder gave me 90 inches of snow before the first of the year.

I did like my Professor/Advisor. He was from St. Louis and had the "you know what's" to say in the middle of Coors Beer Country that you couldn't make good beer with clean water. Coors advertises to this day that crystal-clear mountain water is what makes it taste good. Rolled up in my advisor's statement were both the Mississippi River and Budweiser Beer. The mid-American heartland vs. the Rockies.

He'd say that to his incoming first-year students at the first lecture. *Chutzpah*.

He counseled me on my course choices, all of which seemed deadly dull. They were studies of the big hitters in 18th and 19th century political science. Gag me with a spoon. Thank God, we studied English translations. He counseled me on the grading of mid-terms and finals, which, oddly enough, was my job, not his. It went this way. "You know that old story about sitting at the foot of a staircase and throwing all the blue books up it? The ones that reached the top steps got A's, and so on down the steps. Well, you can't do that. You have to read them." Drat.

I, too, taught classes but not lecture halls. The students were less interesting than what came to class with them. More than one student had a large, often *mucho* large, dog, usually a herding dog, lying alongside his desk. A few students came to school on horseback. In the '60s, the university still had hitching posts here and there. We were only an hour from Cheyenne, Wyoming, and not much more in

A Long way to Tipperary? Try the Great Plains.

an easterly direction to the kinds of ranches like Yellowstone. The Boulder-Denver Highway, called by Lady Bird Johnson the most beautiful highway in America, dissected an unspoiled America. Antelope herds often flanked a car, giving it a run for its money. Nothing like the Belt Parkway in my hometown of Brooklyn. Now, condos, instead of antelope, run along most of the highway.

This was Boulder, pre-JonBenét Ramsey, a small town that butted up against the Rockies, with a large university run by powerful people with small minds. Because of the university, Boulder was on the hippie-trek west, and there were frequent beatings of the long-haired, scraggly dressed trekkers by cowboy boot-wearing "townies" who sported crew cuts. Some of them were nasty beatings. None of them caused much of a stir around town. Most folks felt the hippies should have known better than to come to town.

The last thing in this travelogue took place on the porch of my little house on the prairie, which it was. The porch looked over the plains at a barely visible town, the setting for Truman Capote's *In Cold Blood*. Its presence made me nervous at night.

Not that I wasn't nervous enough, but another night on the porch, I noticed something odd that drew me away from my fears to the east and towards a post on the patio. It was a spider web. Mind you, I'd seen plenty of spider webs in my time, but not with this spider. I'd already been warned not to walk around without boots on. The rattlesnake was a bonified citizen of Colorado, as was the scorpion. As I closed in on this spider, I noticed the bell on its bottom. OMG, I realized I had another worry; this worry was much closer than Kansas. It was a Black Widow spider.

It dawned on me that maybe I'd had my fill of the west—killer snakes, killer spiders, 90 inches of snow, teenagers who all looked like tryouts for Marlboro commercials pounding on other kids who didn't. I needed an exit strategy. Despite my mother's warning that I'd never finish if I dropped out of my Ph.D. program, I quit. (I hate people who are right . . .) But this was my life, and I wasn't enjoying it. Then the phone rang.

The call was from an uncle by marriage. He had been a bomber pilot during WW II. Having navigated flak-filled skies, one isn't much inhibited by convention. He owned an early '50s Ford that looked very much like the police cars in the early Elliott Ness movies or Bonnie and Clyde's car, sans siren and light. In the rearview mirror, it well could have been an unmarked car, and he reveled in tailing drivers while holding one hand, cupped, up to his mouth as if he were talking into a police radio. Boys will be boys, even as grown-ups.

A confirmed bachelor (at least at this time), he had one of the most unique pick-up techniques ever. He kept a small hammer in his trunk. If he saw a striking woman get out of a parked car, he'd either park behind it or alongside it. Out would come the hammer. He'd lightly tap on the rear light, just enough to crack it. Then he would leave an apology note with contact information under the windshield wiper. It worked like a charm.

He was a bit of a renaissance man, dressed in the most refined styles, which was easy because he and his brother-in-law, my blood uncle, owned a men's clothing store. On nights he had no company, he cooked for himself. He would set a table with a tablecloth, linen napkin, and wine as if he were dining in a fine restaurant.

The clothing store, which had become a chain that began in West Hartford, Connecticut, had been sold, and he ended up in Stamford, Connecticut, using all his talents as an entrepreneur and lothario. One of those talents, or both, saw him rise to the presidency of the Jewish Community Center and campaign manager for Stamford's first and last Jewish mayor. Julius Wilensky was his name. His politics put him well to the right of, let's say, Donald Trump or Genghis Khan. Wilensky won. Hence the phone call.

"Bill, how'd you like to give up that 18th-century political crap and practice real politics?" Given what I've already described about my Ph.D. program, you need no further explanation as to why this question hit me like an unerring arrow. "My guy wants a clean-cut, intelligent person who knows about government. He wants to get the Mafia out of the mayor's office." If one measured my intrigue with the United Way fund-raising thermometer, my intrigue would have blown through the top. He'd cracked my taillight. At the end of the semester, I resigned my teaching assistantship and began the march to Connecticut, many miles away. The drive was like something out of a bad movie. I was in a fantasy until reality hit.

The thought of driving alone, Colorado to Connecticut, unnerved me. During the drive to Colorado, somewhere in the middle of Nebraska or Kansas, I noticed in my rearview mirror the transistor radio I had shelved on the car's back seat ledge had become a lump of red, molten plastic. There were lengths of highway so barren, so empty, so hot that I thought a flat tire would end in death. The police would find my skeleton picked over by vultures. And then there was my car.

My car was a yellow Opal, now only found in Europe. I wish I had it today. It got about 45 mpg. Or it got that when it was running, which had to be always. The car had developed a malfunction. If you turned it off, it wouldn't start without a jump. Period. Think about those barren highways. I didn't have the money to fix it. I needed to solve two problems at once and immediately. Repeat after Forest Gump . . . "stupid is as stupid does."

I put an ad in the university newspaper for someone who needed a ride east over winter break. This co-pilot would share the driving (Boulder to Stamford is 1,831 miles or 27 hours, depending on how many stops the flying crow makes and how long his wings stay folded). Whoever was not driving could sleep or run in and buy snacks and drinks. There would always be someone in the car while the other used the restrooms. In ways I hadn't even thought of, overnight would prove challenging.

●●●

The ad was answered. Let's say my automobile roomie wasn't someone I would have picked. He was thin as Ichabod Crane, though not as tall. He had long, blond hair that looked like he used chicken fat to condition it. There was an odor that spoke of long stints in-between showers. He had the personality of a gray stone wall. Since he was the one and only respondent, he became my copilot.

My next indication of "bad choice" was the joint he lit up as soon as we crossed the Boulder city line. I explained what job I was about to take, that a drug bust wouldn't sit well with my mayor, that I couldn't breathe, and that I'd rather he not be high when it was his turn to drive. He showed no interest. He showed so little interest at times I wondered if he was alive. It was freezing cold. The Opal's little heater was no match for mid-west winter. It began to snow as the sun started to set. Soon the highway narrowed to one lane, and our speed dropped to 35 mph. At this rate, I figured in rudimentary math, it might take three months to get to Stamford. Besides, as many of you know, driving in a snowstorm is exhausting. We had to stop.

The blinking "rooms available" sign was attached to what could have been the Bates Motel, but it wasn't as fancy. Low on money, we could afford only one room. I made a decision because he was incapable of making one. I'd fill up the car, hide it, engine running, in the lot, and hope God loved me. In the room, Mr. *Eau de* Chicken Fat had zero interest in the room's shower. He had in a suitcase some stuff I'd never seen. It was white and powdery. Desperate for sleep, I turned the lights out during a rant triggered by the white powder, a rant that got worse until it reached a fever pitch. He'd lie down, jump up, curse at no one, curse at me, and throw his clothes across the room. Maybe it was the Bates Motel.

He finally fell asleep. I made another decision. With the blaring of his snoring to cover me, I scooped up my few belongings and fled. It was a "pay first, then you get the key" kind of motel. I didn't have to check out, just leave. God did love me. While still freezing cold, it had stopped snowing, and the car was still there, puttering like a motorboat from which lifted puffs of environmentally bad exhaust. Off I went.

"Writing is a socially acceptable form of getting naked in public."

– Paulo Coelho

"And by the way, everything in life is writable about if you have the outgoing guts to do it, and the imagination to improvise. The worst enemy to creativity is self-doubt."

– Sylvia Plath, *The Unabridged Journals of Sylvia Plath*

Connecticut

STAMFORD

There is nothing so exhilarating as being shot at . . .
and realizing they missed." — Winston Churchill

Old Town Hall Stamford, Connecticut.

●●●

When I got to Stamford, to my pre-rented apartment, I felt like the crow did not have one more feather to donate to this misadventure. I was happier than I'd ever been to see a shower and stayed in it longer than I've probably ever stayed in a shower since. After that, my uncle by marriage, who lived one floor down, had me as dinner company, linen tablecloth, wine glasses, fancy plates, and then to bed, I went. The next day would be a press conference and my first day as the executive aide to the mayor of Connecticut's fourth-largest city.

As far as fish size and ponds go, I was a bigger fish in a bigger pond. This position suited me well. I had long ago decided with Machiavelli that being the kingmaker was better than being the king. I wasn't the kingmaker, but I was the king's representative and one of his *consiglieres*. The king said, "do it." I saw that it got done, when it got done, and by whom. Suddenly, a lot of people knew who I was. I had credentials. I had a "courtesy card" introducing me as a "personal friend" of the police chief. I even bought myself a large flashlight with a red flasher that I could put on my dashboard in case I had to get somewhere fast. My car was now a fake cop car. As I said, boys will be boys . . . It was totally illegal, but then again, I was a personal friend of the police chief. This was going to be fun, or so I thought. As it turned out, I lasted two years. I then became the Deputy Director of the city's anti-poverty agency and, finally, the executive director of the largest multi-modality drug/alcohol treatment facility in southern Connecticut. In its fight bag, it had a 40-bed residential treatment program.

Social life? I had none. My misery and the advent of computer dating coincided, so I joined a dating club. I hit it off with a girl. My luck, she was in Boston. After several lengthy, engaging, and intriguing computer conversations, we exchanged phone numbers and addresses. She had this very sultry voice and a penchant for the salacious. Remember, no cell phones, no selfies. We had no idea what we looked like, but like each other, we seemed to. I invited her to Stamford, which gave her the unspoken understanding of a sleepover. I was psyched, as we said way back when. Psyched out was what I got.

The building I lived in had an *avant-garde* design. The elevator left you in a mini lobby, the exit door opening onto a catwalk to all the apartments on the floor. I pulled out all the stops. I cooked up a storm, the *pièce de résistance* of which was a two-and-a-half-pound lobster. I'd gone to the wine shop to select an appropriate wine. Those were the days when *Mateus*, a Portuguese rose dressed in a straw-encased bottle, was the thing to drink. Anyone who thought themselves cool not only drank *Mateus* but, when finished, stuck a candle in the bottle's cork hole and created wax drippings a la Jackson Pollack.

I was in a fever, in constant prep motion. When prepping was done, I stayed in motion, pacing around the apartment. I was so startled when the security alarm rang, even though I was expecting her, that I seemed to have come apart at the seams, with pieces of me flying around like I was a thousand-piece jigsaw puzzle knocked off the table.

I couldn't contain myself. Sensing how long the elevator would take, I peeked out my door, about five apartments from where she would set foot onto the catwalk. It took one glance to know I was now trapped. I don't know what I was imagining, but she wasn't it. She was short and stout. Her hair looked like she was wearing a fright wig, and she was moving towards me like a woman on a mission. I shut the door. How was I to get out of this? "Why?" you ask.

A lot of it was her perfume. It was so thick that it enveloped her body in a cloud. It got to the apartment before she did. Not even the air-conditioner could disperse it; I feared the perfume might clog it. As the aromas of dinner began to waft into the dining room, they mingled with her "*eau de* whatever" creating a choking smog that settled over the dinner table. And this was but the beginning of the evening.

Over dinner, her sultry voice now seemed husky. Her suggestive comments were no longer intriguing or attractive. I gallantly did the dishes, hoping for inspiration. She dashed into the bedroom and returned in a teddy-type nighty. She was ready for bear—me. My first savior was the TV. We watched it. She snuggled up to me, getting as close as the perfume cloud would allow. But bedtime came. It was time for a miracle. Then God took pity on me. The phone rang. It wasn't

God, but the idea I got was heaven-inspired. I forget who was on the phone; that person must have thought me insane. I manufactured a conversation, just like you see on TV, responding to a voice that was having a completely different conversation. In the mix were mystery and urgency. "Yes, I know where it is. He did what? And the mayor said for me to handle it. I'm on it."

As I hurriedly dressed, I had to fill in the pseudo-conversation to make an explanation. Yes, it was an emergency. No, I couldn't tell her; it was confidential. When the mayor says jump, all you do is ask how high. 'sounded to me like it might take all night. I apologized, told her to sleep well, have breakfast, and that I'd be in touch. When I returned home, all that remained was the finally dissipating perfume cloud.

Every year, during the Jewish New Year, every Jew is bound to ask forgiveness for ills done to others. There is a wide range of prayers to help one do that, to atone, which is why Yom Kippur is known as "The Day of Atonement." Not only did I offer atonement that year, but I did for many years after. And so came and went my social life.

Aside from my two male friends already mentioned, I had two more. One was an African American detective. Jeremiah was not a bull frog. He was a former football star and, although in his forties, still looked like he could bowl over linemen. He took me on as a project, teaching me the layout of the city, which neighborhoods held trouble and what kind, and which didn't. The most prescient thing he ever said to me was, "Don't let the glass buildings, the rolling green neighborhoods, the fact that Jackie Robinson's widow lives here make you forget what I'm about to tell you. There are people in this town who would shoot you, or me, if they saw us riding together." Gulp. From then until now, I became a big proponent of watching my back, or, as they say in law enforcement and the military, of having "the six" of my buddies.

From the other friend, I had no such deep conversations. We met at a dude ranch and got a kick out of each other. One night he had a party and invited me to come early to his near Prospect Park apartment to help set up. We went to the supermarket and did what they do at the Seattle Seafood Market before I knew there was such a place, no less what made it famous. That would be throwing fish across the market, a quarterback spiraling a mackerel to his receiver at the cash register. The culmination was this. He picked up a melon and said, "Go deep!" I ran a pass route through several aisles when he let loose the melon. Fortunately, it flew into my outstretched hands.

The management let us pay for our goods before they threw us out.

I was never into drugs, especially after running an anti-drug agency. For reasons long forgotten, I decided to get a roommate. Maybe it would give me extra spending money; perhaps it would reduce the loneliness. My choice was a guy who recently got back from a tour in Vietnam. I didn't know, but he was a big-time pothead. His idea of conversation was getting high and telling me about shooting monkeys out of trees and watching enemy soldiers get torn apart by claymore mines. I had, in high school, one joint. It turned my throat into a furnace; I coughed relentlessly.

I told my roomie I couldn't smoke because it ripped up my throat. He had a solution. He went to the fridge and got an apple. Then he cored it, putting aluminum foil with holes punched in it in the hole at the top. He jabbed a pipe stem through the apple's middle. The weed went on the top, cradled in the aluminum. A match did the rest. Handing his creation to me, the Monkey Murderer's instructions were to draw the smoke in through the pipe stem. The apple's taste and moisture would soften the smoke's harshness. By golly, it worked. It worked so well that I thought I might have to increase my purchases of apples. Please don't tell anyone I told you how to do this . . .

Back to Prospect Park. My grocery store quarterback had a hookah in his apartment. I'd never seen one, and my only familiarity with the term was its Brooklyn pronunciation which meant prostitute. There was more education coming. This time, one smokes through water vapor instead of apple cores. It's like, "A spoonful of sugar makes the medicine go down." He told me he had switched "meds" and that instead of pot, he had put "hash" (hashish) in the hookah.

That meant nothing to me. We passed the hash around the party for several hours, sitting like Turks without turbans, until I had to go. I had the sometimes perilous ride on the Hutchinson River and Merritt Parkways to negotiate. I got up to say my goodbyes to find that I couldn't get up. The floor wouldn't remain horizontal under my feet. My friend walked me to my car, assuming fresh air would resolve the problem. He was wrong.

A word about my car: I was now driving a three-cycle Saab. The oil and gas went in together. The seats had mattress springs in them, or so it seemed. Hit a bump, and you'd likely hit the roof if your seatbelt was not tightly fastened. The mileage it got to a gallon of gas was so high that there'd be block-long lines around Saab dealerships if they were still in production. I got in, started the car, and negotiated myself out of Brooklyn. Then it began.

I had this sense my seat was rising towards the roof. Ahhh, I now understood the word high. I was fighting to keep myself where I should have been in the driver's seat. I pushed myself down and inadvertently also pushed down the gas pedal. The car leaped forward so suddenly I thought I'd ended up in the back seat. On occasion, I'd miss the gas and hit the brake. Had I been watched from a police helicopter; the cops would have seen a halting motion to my forward progress. I knew I was high; if I got a DUI, being a hotshot would come to a screeching halt. I had to get home and do it under the radar, no pun intended. Awww hell. Pun definitely intended.

I rolled down the front windows; I pulled into a gas station and rolled down the back ones. I headed out again, sober enough to realize that I was freezing to death. Before that happened, my high became lower, and with great relief, I returned safely and at ground level to my monkey-shooting roommate.

A word about him and my social life. War does terrible things to people, including the survivors. I don't think my roomie had PTSD, but he was warped. He had no regard for another's feelings. This extended to his dating. His idea of dating was sort of like his shooting monkeys out of trees. Every girl was a target. He did fabulously with two broad categories of girls. One was the girl who wanted to walk on the wild side before she had the perfect wedding and her perfect 2.5 children while driving the latest model perfect car. The other group of girls were just like him.

I had met such a girl. In a hard looking way, she was stunning. A Playboy bunny figure poured into anything tight. What did Jerry Lee Lewis intone? "Breathless." That's what she made me. As George Jones crooned, I had a slow hand. We dated, we got very passionate, but we hadn't yet consummated the relationship. One night she came to see me and met the monkey-shooter. Before the night was out, they were in bed together, and I was left twiddling the thumbs on my slow hands. Such was life in Stamford.

BACK TO WORK

Not long after I started, I discovered that the rumors were true. The Mafia was entrenched in Connecticut and Stamford. Yes, my uncle had referred to it with the job offer. Some things happened that showed me that the Mafia was not passing through; it had stopped at city hall and even at my desk. Read on.

The Mafia was a concept to me. When my uncle mentioned it, I thought he meant the standard brand of corrupt officials. Of course, I was aware that there was such a thing. It was a particularly bloody time as struggles for power pitted some Mafia families against others. There was evidence of their influence not far from my Brooklyn neighborhood.

Down from me on Ocean Parkway in Brooklyn was where several high-ranking Mafioso from the Columbo family lived. One day, the neighborhood's Italian church's gold and be-jeweled statue of Mother Mary disappeared. It was hugely expensive, really priceless. The local precinct threw everything they had at solving the crime but to no avail. One of the family members, also a member of the church, suggested to the captain that they lay off for a few weeks—sort of a capo-to-captain chat. If the statue didn't return in three weeks, the cops could make a go at it again. In less than three weeks, there she was one morning, sitting pretty in her honored place. But someone from the neighborhood was missing. This was not a movie.

Not from Brooklyn, but you get the idea.

●●●

When I got to Stamford and settled in, I learned that the city garage and building department were "Mafia territory." This meant I would inevitably have my day with them. It began when the foreman of the garage called and asked me to lunch. He then took me on a tour of the facility. Neither lunch nor the garage was anything special. My host, who looked like an overgrown teddy bear, spoke in soft tones, albeit the words and accent were pretty coarse. His name? Tony, of course. Tony became my link to the family, and frankly, legal, or not, he did some really good stuff for me. Let's start with the circus.

The mayor decided it would be good politics to do something for the inner city. I think he began to realize that even though the currently called ghetto was the neighborhood in which he grew up, it had changed over the last fifty years. On an inner city tour I gave him, we came to a large, vintage corner house with a big wrap-around porch. He said, "That's the house in which I grew up. What're they complaining about?" I explained that there were likely eight families now in residence. The spacious rooms had been chopped up and reconfigured. It was on the building code department's violation list. Response? "Well, we took care of it; why don't they?" Exasperated, I had no answer.

The newspapers, radio, and TV were awash with ads that the circus was coming to Madison Square Garden. The mayor told me to get five buses and take as many kids as would fit in them. The buses were the easy part. Call a few bus companies, compare prices, and sign a contract. It's only now I wonder why we weren't required to call for bids on the contract. As it says on the law shows, never ask a question to which you don't want the answer. Here's why.

The hard part was the money. Five buses, tickets, money for snacks. It would cost thousands of dollars, not one of which was in the budget. The closer we got to the date, the sweatier my palms got. Our Corporation Council, Frankie D'Angelo, kept telling me, "Stop worrying. It will show up."

It did.

One morning I got in early, and it seemed that as soon as I approached the side of the desk on which sat the telephone, it rang. There was a muffled voice on the other end. "You want money to get them (n-word in the plural) to the circus?" it wheezed. "Yes," I stammered. "And who is this?" That went unanswered. The voice, said, "Look in your desk." The next sound I heard was "click," as the line went dead. I pulled open my desk drawer to find a very pregnant envelope. It contained a ton of money, a lot more than I needed. Another thought. How did someone get into my office? As a matter of fact, how did someone get into the mayor's suite to get into my office? I was the first to arrive that morning. Another question smartly not asked.

The trip went as smoothly as any trip with 200-plus kids in their middle school years could. The only problem was that the envelope still had money in it after the accounting. I took the envelope into the mayor's office and asked him where the extra dough should go. Loud protestations met me. "I don't know nothin' about any money! Don't even bring that envelope into this office! Get outta here!" This mayor was not a John Lindsey Republican from the silk-stocking district of Manhattan. He was a poor kid from a poor family who worked his way up at Yale Lock. The spoken tongue wasn't his strong suit.

Back in the drawer went the money. Every time I looked at it, I wondered when the FBI would show up for a chat. I discussed it with Frankie. His advice? Spend it. Get a nice suit, a pair of shoes, and some shirts. Frankie was a major-league dresser. Me? How could I do that? With it in my pocket, the money, I'm sure, would have produced a neon arrow pointing to me that said, ARREST HIM!" There the money lay—for a year. Finally, I said, "What the hell!" and did what D'Angelo suggested. Neither the arrow nor the FBI ever showed up.

Tony did me another solid. We received a Federal grant for our Neighborhood Youth Corps program. It was to keep kids off the summer streets by finding jobs for which the employer wouldn't have to pay. Only one place could accommodate that goal and allow 50 or so Black teenage males into their domain. It was the city garage. Tony said, "Send 'em to me. We'll let 'em ride around on the back of garbage trucks all summer, and don't worry—they won't get into any trouble." Given who he was, I could take that to the bank. Chalk up another success story.

The next favor came from one of our periodic lunches. Floyd Patterson was the rage, and we talked about his up-and-coming fight at the Garden. Tony asked, "'ever seen a prize fight?" I had not, except on TV. "I got an extra ticket. Wanna go? "

What a night!

The last interface I had with the Mafia was after I left the mayor's office and worked at the local anti-poverty agency. And it was a doozy. The director, an Italian, with a Master of Social Work (MSW), had two problems. One rumor had it that he had embezzled several hundred thousand dollars. The second, no rumor at all, was that his stunningly beautiful wife was cheating on him. There's a certain

The Gentleman of Boxing: World Champ Floyd Patterson

simpatico between Jews and Italians of the same age. We became good friends. One night over a beer, he lent me his MSW, leaned back, and let it all out to me. It was about his wife. A lot of what he said was code: honor, face, and the roles of men and women in a family. These were tenets of the Mafia, so it didn't surprise me when he told me that his uncle was a mafia captain in the Bridgeport area (captains in the mafia are usually killers and/or the guys who choose the killers). He felt he had no choice but to have his uncle put out a contract on his wife. That meant, in simple English, he was going to have her killed.

I must admit, as that came rushing with the power and speed of a river rapids-worth of words, my reaction was, "Holy S##t!" I said nothing. Dropping the MSW role and switching to *consigliere,* I began to reason with him. It wouldn't be long before he became the first suspect. Husbands always are. Tracing his relationship to his uncle wouldn't take too long. Conspiracy to commit murder could put him in jail for life. Wasn't divorce an easier, safer, more intellectual way to go? I won. For days I was quaking. I had had a conversation that would determine if someone lived or died. I wasn't sure that was in my job description, nor if I had the constitution for it to be. I gave myself an A.

There was to be another Floyd Patterson connection in my life. Patterson's sparring partner lived in Stamford. He had a job in one of the poverty agency's programs. A gentle giant, he walked slowly and talked slowly, probably from being hit in the head a zillion times. He became another unlikely friend for a skinny middle-class kid from Brooklyn who'd never made or used a fist in anger. He was about 5'10" tall, easily weighed 230 or 240, and nowhere on his body, except maybe his head, could you poke and find soft tissue. He was a black boulder.

He was drunk and having a tantrum inside the program's office. Some voice in his head convinced him he hadn't been paid and that there was a conspiracy to take advantage of him. The chief of police wanted me to talk him down lest they have to shoot him. This could have been TV, me walking up to the second floor at 2 a.m. and entering a room with a roaring replica of Mighty Joe Young. I didn't think he'd hurt me, but he had done something just before I arrived that gave me pause. He had picked up the steel floor safe in both his hands and threw it through the window, taking part of the inside and outside building wall with it. The safe, and wall splinters, greeted me on the sidewalk as I jumped from my car. It was awe-inspiring. And fear-inducing. BTW, that big flashlight with the red blinking light I mentioned? I used it that night.

It ended well. It's a great story for, let's say a book . . . It's also something that had I a few more years on me, I'd never have done.

A man of superior intellect and savvy now ran the anti-poverty agency. How do I assess that? He chose me as his #2 . . . I was the only white person in a senior staff position, and my learning curve was off the charts. It started with this caution. "Don't ever say around here that you're not prejudiced. It's bulls##t! Everyone has prejudices about one thing or another. If you deny prejudice, the staff and the community will sideline you as another white do-gooder, and you won't last very long."

That was the beginning of my immersion in the world of Black people. Besides Jeremiah, I knew I would need someone who wasn't my boss to guide me through this. That mentor came along in the person of a young black woman, a single parent, who had enrolled in one of our new programs. It taught elementary job interview skills like buying an alarm clock, setting an alarm clock, "acceptable" ways to do hair and makeup, and what to wear and what not to wear. The girl had a good enough heart not to want me to make a fool of myself.

Over a span of weeks, we talked about everything black. Then she invited me to Sunday dinner at her grandma's. The grapevine had put out the word—this white guy had something good about him. How did they know? Grandma suffered no fools. Grandma and the girl's aunt became coaches on the white kid's team. Pork was for dinner, and I learned, "Poor folks use every part of the pig except the oink." I learned the hierarchal courtesies of the black community and family life. Grandmas were the queens. I learned to talk less and listen more and never to make a promise or offer I could not keep. There was also Auntie, who owned a hair salon and suggested I spend some time in her shop and listen in on what could have been the Black Wives of Stamford, Connecticut. I learned about braiding (platting) hair and began getting my hair cut there. Word went through the community like wildfire.

Learning abounds in a new environment. One of my colleagues drank scotch and milk. To me, that was a gross abuse of a great liquor. To him, it made gastric sense: "The milk coats your stomach, the scotch absorbs more slowly, and the evening lasts longer." I couldn't get past the combination to test the concoction and come to a decision. Michael, who had a beautiful, long-suffering wife, was a serial cheater. He began to see himself as a caricature of "Sportin' Life" in *Porgy and Bess*. He needed more milk and less scotch added to his personality. He became a Muslim, his wife did too, and near as I could tell, they lived happily ever after.

One learns and grows if one watches and listens. One of my colleagues was anti-school busing. I couldn't understand it given the options. He explained: "How would you like to live in a crappy neighborhood, put your kids on a bus, have them watch through the windows as the bus passed through neighborhoods they'd never be able to live in, and do it twice a day?" Hmmm . . . 'never thought of it that way, did I? Suddenly, neighborhood schools made a lot of sense.

Came a day when another co-worker, Don, was walking to work, as he did every day because he had no car. I passed him, honked, drew his attention, and waved. When he got to work, I said, as if I should get a prize, "Did you see me wave to you? He said, "I did. That was nice. It would've been nicer if you'd stopped and given me a lift." It was another Hmmm moment. I realized I'd never even thought about stopping. I came to understand it was a form of built-in racism. Pick up a scruffy-looking black guy with a beard, wearing army fatigues and unlaced combat boots that looked very the worse for wear? *That's what buses are for*—would be a white person's thought. The missing thought was, *if you had the money to take the bus.*

"Oh, now I see," said the blind man.

And then there was the conversation with my office mate about our domestic goals for the future. We had some downtime and were musing over where our lives would take us. The question was, "If you could live anywhere, where would it be?" I had a hard time answering because my choices were almost unlimited. His answer was quick and pointed, "Scarsdale—with only black people." Scarsdale is a toney, mostly white, suburb near New York City.

One night, I was invited to a basement party. That would be a party held in a basement . . . I would be the only white person. When I walked in, there was a bit of a minor break in the action. It was the "hi's" from some of the partiers. Everyone knew who I was; that I had Grandma's seal of approval. I realized her granddaughter's training had succeeded.

Then there came the sit-in that tested all of this groundwork. As my grandma would say, "Something to write home about." It was the sit-in that jolted me from the mayor's office and jettisoned me into the anti-poverty agency. Even though I was there, there were parts of this I am hard-pressed to believe. The mayor was leaving. He asked me to attend a meeting held by black organizations about the housing situation in town. I might have been Executive Aide to the Mayor, and it may have been a strong mayor system, but I didn't plan or build houses. I did give commitments that I thought I could get the mayor to buy into. It was a hot meeting, and I left with scorch marks on my butt and my ego. But it was the reason for what came next.

It was hard times and unrest in the Black community that knitted organizations into a Black Power Movement. The Black Panthers were chief among them. One day an activist organization of Black women called the Welfare Rights Mothers sent a dozen or more of its members to hold a sit-in at the mayor's office for more affordable housing and several other items. The housing meeting had triggered the sit-in. The commitments I fought for had gone largely unmet. How the group got to the fifth floor of city hall, I don't know. My secretary knocked at my door and said, "You'd better come see this." We peeked into the mayor's conference room, and there they were, accompanied by several local Black leaders, some from the Panthers, and some from other groups. I went into the mayor's office to tell him what was transpiring. He was on his way out. It was the annual politicians' pick-nik of The Marching Clam and Chowder Society, an event he never missed. (Don't ask. It's some northeastern political nonsense.) I tried to talk some sense into him. His retort? Call the police, and when they get here, tell them I said to throw the intruders out the window. He was not kidding.

In minutes, the cavalry arrived, led by the estimable Capt. Potts who had a belly to warrant the name. He said, "I heard the mayor wants them thrown out the window. I can do that, but now you are in charge, kid. What do you want me to do?" Out the window was not an option, and I knew Potts well enough to know it wasn't for him either. I said I wanted to try something and walked into the room that had swelled with the addition of his detail. I dragged another chair in and sat down. I decided whatever I thought of saying would be better said sitting with them than standing over them.

Telling those assembled I wanted this to end peacefully and with satisfaction, I tried my first gambit. I said, "Everyone carrying a weapon of any kind, put it on the table." There was some grumbling, but then an astonishing number of weapons hit the well-polished, long, wooden conference table. Zip guns, real guns, knives of several sorts, and a few pairs of brass knuckles joined the pile. I realized the room and residents were much more dangerous than they had appeared. Potts said cops don't give up guns, but he did remove the officers from the room, leaving with a stage whisper, "We'll be right outside." I don't remember if he ended that with an "if" or a "when" you need me.

My second gambit was to listen. I said I wanted everyone at the table who had something to say to have the chance to say it. I took notes and asked one of the interlopers to do so. That way, my report with theirs would accurately reflect the demands.

The outpourings began. Some were very angry, some worrisomely angry, some heartrendingly sad, some almost professorial. Stories abounded about sick children in buildings with no heat, dangerous conditions in public housing, and a host more one can still read about in today's news from around the country. Such stories can be a cold glass of water splashed in the face. I was determined to let everyone have their say; if someone talked too long, I'd let the group take care of their own. I decided to order dinner for everyone and figured the money would show up again from someone from somewhere sometime. It did.

The next morning, the mayor returned to work seemingly sated with Clam Chowder doings. His conference room, he noted snidely, was still occupied. He had seen neither bodies on the sidewalk nor any broken windows. The mayor flashed a look of anger; Potts shrugged it off.

It took twenty-three hours. Nothing worse than yelling and occasionally screaming took place. We had agreed on a list of "demands," of which there were a dozen or more. I signed it; they signed it and left. I was hero material in the corporate board rooms, men who did not want a race riot in town, and the leadership of the Black community who also didn't want one. With pride and trepidation,

I took the "contract" to the mayor only to discover my hero status disappeared 20-30 feet from my office. He scanned it. He uttered some unmentionable phrases and clauses and then said, "I thought I told you to throw them out of the windows." I was again speechless. He filled my verbal vacuum with this: "You got your choice—resign or be fired. Either way, you're out of here tomorrow." Heroism, as we know, can be costly. I hadn't lost any body parts or my life, but I now had no job. Thankfully, the community paid me its thanks. Remember our poster boy for conjuring up a conspiracy to commit murder? He had been fired, and the new director asked me if I would be his deputy. The rent would get paid.

We accomplished a lot. We even got to check off a few of those demands, but a different gun from a different group further changed my perspective. My new boss wanted to show me the inner city at night shortly after I began my job. As I was to learn during the child murders in Atlanta (foreshadowing, folks), once the clock strikes midnight, you should be home. It's a different world. Maybe that's why they call it the dead of night.

After seeing some of the "sights," we pulled into a parking lot and found we were in another kind of site, a gun site. We had driven right into a steel-jacketed spat between two gangs. When my boss identified himself from behind a car, a sound I'll never forget met him, the sound of a bullet cutting air. I asked my tour guide what had just flown over our heads. He told me, ". . . a bullet. The M . . . F'ers . . . just took a shot at us." In times like that, some say the mind becomes as clear as freshly windexed windows. In small electric letters, my brain produced a quote from Winston Churchill: "There is no better feeling than to be shot at—and realize that they missed."

We got into the car and fled.

I told you about my young Black mentor and her grandmother. We were supposed to meet up for dinner, but she never showed up. I caught up with her a few days later and got an explanation. She had joined the Black Panthers and had gone to New Haven to a protest rally. Things went sideways very quickly. Shots were fired.

She had shot a cop, fortunately not hurting him seriously, and then left Bridgeport to go into hiding.

One finds in life certain signs that flash red. If you are smart, you recognize the danger. Some have different amounts of space between them. If you are really smart, you know not to cross them. Having a gun moll as a friend was my line. I would not ignore them. What would I do now?

Ever hear the expression, "Better lucky than good?" Well, just as lucky timing enabled my transition from the mayor's office to the anti-poverty agency, luck struck true for me again. The agency had started a drug treatment program. It had bitten off more than it could chew trying to run it. It wanted to incorporate and spin it off as its own non-profit. The board asked me to be its executive director; I accepted. For senior staff, I hired a specialist in adolescent psychology and a recovered addict who had graduated from a large, well-respected program in New York that still exists. One day in discussing psychology, the doctor uttered this memorable line: "Normal adolescents are abnormal." Anyone who's raised teens knows that.

The recovered addict would be the director of services, the doc would be the medical director, and I would be the executive director. We worked as a triumvirate. Once again, I had landed on a planet foreign to me. I didn't take drugs and did not know much about them. What I did know was how to run an organization. My *tour de force* ended after two years. But I went out in style. It ended after an argument with none other than the state's governor, but we're not there yet.

One meets an interesting variety of people in a drug treatment facility, especially in programs with different treatment modalities. In-patient, outpatient, methadone, and alcohol treatment were all in our treatment quiver. Active addicts, I learned, can't be trusted. It's not because they don't want to be—they can't help themselves. I've learned that unless someone is clean for five or more years, there's at least a 50-50 chance they will relapse and hence shouldn't be blindly trusted. That's called recidivism. Shunning for five years isn't the answer. Not putting them in a situation where the temptation is so great that they'll end up saying, "The devil made me do it," is the right approach.

If nothing else, addicts develop a great number of survival talents. One day I was frantic. My wife was having labor pains. I lived 35 miles from work and had locked my keys in the car. "No sweat!" said one of the guys. He'd opened the car in less time than it took me to say, "How on earth did you do that?"

One day, I wandered out of the office into the back of the residential treatment program to watch some of the guys play basketball and maybe get into the game. One of our patients was about 6'5" tall. I swear to you, no matter where he was on the court, he did not miss a shot. I learned why. He had been a highly touted high school baller, got a scholarship to college, and was a sure pro draft pick. But dope turned him into a dope. He went to jail before he ever stepped onto an NBA court. And now, years later, here he was, fighting his battle towards recovery but never having lost that golden touch. Sometimes, addicts can't live with who they've become when shooting up and what they did to support their habits. My sure-shot client killed himself after "graduating" from the program. He had agreed to a certain amount of outpatient counseling. One day he didn't show up.

In the drug world, very few of the sad stories become ones with happy endings.

We had patients give birth to addicted babies and patients whose addiction severely affected their deliveries and their children's health. One story tells it all.

A woman who lived on the same block as the treatment center came flying into the lobby. Her screeching, squalling, and caterwauling preceded her. "IT'S GONE!" she wailed. "IT'S GONE!"

The woman was the great-granddaughter of slaves. When her family was "decommissioned," the plantation owner gave them a set of sterling silver as an I'm sorry and good luck gift. The silver had passed from generation to generation. They used it. They never sold it, even though the money could have changed their circumstances. It was their symbol of freedom. Then fortune turned its face away. The son was a patient of ours. His mother knew the silver was in grave jeopardy. One day when the boy was in residence with us, the woman, with friends, one of whom probably ratted her out later for some dope, dug up her floor. They created a deep hole. In it, she buried her treasure. They smoothed out the floor, poured concrete to fill the hole. Over it, she put a rug.

Every drug-infested neighborhood has an operation that takes stolen goods for a pittance and fences them. During the 'fifties and 'sixties there were still little trucks that toured neighborhoods to polish silverware and sharpen knives. Some enterprising, heartless man had taken one of them, removed the machinery that drove the sharpening and polishing elements, and put in a smelter. He would give the addict pennies on the dollar, and in minutes, whatever it was he acquired became an untraceable lump of metal, which he, in turn, would sell.

The heirloom silver that had survived emancipation, reconstruction, and segregation was gone for a few tiny balls of crack. It broke my heart when she finally managed to cough and cry out the story. I wanted to kill the kid because, with that act, he and his mother had nothing. They not only lost their history, but they also lost their insurance. Yes, we had the son arrested, and yes, it led to the arrest of the smelter, but no, it didn't bring back the silver. The addict and their addictions have tentacles whose reach can be far, wide, and even be deadly.

And then there was the governor, Tom Meskill, a Republican remake of Napoleon in size and temperament. Nixon had become president. He changed the formula for the distribution of federal money that had previously flowed from federal to local. Now it flowed from federal to state. They were called block grants and were in the hands of politicians, not local non-profits. In that change, we lost a significant source of funding. I appealed to our congressman. I spoke to the mayor and city council members, including a friend, who became the savior of BJ Thomas (more foreshadowing). And yes, the Mafia. There was no recourse left but the governor.

Stamford was at the bottom of the state, and Hartford, the state capital, was at the top. I was able to make an appointment. On the drive up, I had plenty of time to think of what I would say and how many things could go wrong. The nerves hit me when I walked into the state capitol building. This was a whole 'nother league than Stamford's city hall. I felt like a hand had grabbed my throat and begun to squeeze. Had I been living with my mother or even had a girlfriend with good taste, I would have known not to wear what I wore to see this very conservative governor. What did I wear? Not wing tips, but shoe boots, not a suit but slacks, not a tie and jacket but the fashion rage of the day, a Nehru jacket. I had dressed for the wrong meeting. Thank God, I wasn't wearing a dashiki and beads.

The conversation didn't begin with much cordiality. In the governor's eyes, I was a young punk speaking on behalf of other young punks who were addicts and criminals. It is one thing to speak truth to power. It is another thing when power doesn't care. The governor didn't care.

I began in this restrictive atmosphere where I could hardly get my chest to draw in air. "Governor Meskill . . ." I made my pitch. I don't remember much until the end when he came at me with lines about the destruction of society as we know it. Sound familiar? It was ridiculous and hit a nerve. Had I gone with an older, established politician, things, except the final result, would have gone differently. But I hadn't; I was alone. Suddenly, I became some ventriloquist's dummy as my mouth began to operate on its own.

This is how it went. The governor said something pretty racist and culturally damning. Instead of charmingly telling him I was sure he didn't mean that, I hit him with a broadside fired like it was from the Battleship *Missouri*. Direct hit. He bellowed, "DO YOU KNOW WHO I AM?" Of course, I did, so I told him. "You're Governor Thomas Meskill, and I don't care who you are. You shouldn't say things like that."

Governors aren't spoken to like that—by anyone. Angry, even enraged, he stood up (which was hard to tell . . .) behind his huge, wooden, historic desk. He was apoplectic. Not only was he being spoken to like that, but he was also being spoken to like that by some kid representing those he saw as turning society onto its head. The man was so mad, I thought he might have a stroke.

This retort came like flames spat from a dragon's mouth: "You're damn well right. I'm the governor, and I could have you dragged out of here in handcuffs by the state police!" Uh oh. Suddenly I felt the ice beginning to crack under my feet, so when he continued, "GET OUTTA HERE BEFORE I DO!" I took him up on his "suggestion," grabbed my case, and fled. My mission was a failure. I drove back to Stamford thinking everytime I saw a cop, I thought he was coming for me. Thomas Meskill became a judge, and I thought my time in Connecticut was nearly done. It seemed best to look for a job while I still had one. "Seek, and ye shall find." I did find, and that's how Atlanta, Georgia, became my next stop. But just before that, I learned I wasn't a businessman.

My city councilman friend, who was to become my best friend, could talk an Eskimo into buying ice, and was a whiz at mathematical conceptions. He had established a business that would handle financial issues for companies. His wrinkle? The computer. Look at your iPad, desktop, or phone when you read this. His computer was about 6 feet tall. Its width was wider than an NBA player's wingspan. This beast was so big it had to have its own room. It also had to have its own air conditioning system because of the heat it gave off. It needed a nanny to make sure it was all right. When one walked into the reception area and saw this "thing" through the glass windows of its office, it was nothing short of impressive; yet, it was slower and had less storage than any of the three items I mentioned above, and it cost a bloody fortune to run. It couldn't do half of what an iPhone does. Yet compared to a group of employees doing the same tasks with calculators and early edition desktops, it was lightning in a bottle or room.

Before we go further, let's get Mr. "Raindrops Keep Fallin'on my head" out of the way. BJ had finished a concert in Stamford and proceeded to get both high as a kite and arrested. His manager called my friend, my friend called me, I called the Chief, and Thomas was spirited out of Stamford and back to New York City. With nery a thank you, an autograph, or even a gift 45, I might add.

Back to the office. It soon became apparent that the costs of his new worker bee would be astronomical. It ate up electricity like kids eat Halloween candy. Add the air-conditioning costs to keep it cool. More for it to eat (business) was the answer. Thus, was born the idea of developing a mini conglomerate around the computer. He asked me to form a polling company that would do market research for businesses and political polling for politicians. Opinion, Incorporated came to life. Not a bad name, if I say so myself. I studied polling in college. Terrified of numbers, I never took statistics. How was I going to analyze the product? I could write the questions, supervise the pollsters, and look for clients. The rest? That was a problem. We decided to hire someone and ended up capturing more lightning in another bottle. A young man doing statistical analysis for one of the premier polling companies in the world wanted to work in a small company where he could have more influence. I would now look for business, and he would do everything else. Whew!

"Oh, you hate your job? Why didn't you say so? There's a support group for that. It's called everybody, and they meet at the bar."

— **Drew Carey**, Comedian,
Talk Show Host

"Doing nothing is very hard to do . . . you never know when you're finished."

— **Leslie Nielsen**,
Comedian and Actor

Book Two

The AJC Years

"Substitute 'damn' every time you're inclined to write 'very;' your editor will delete it and the writing will be just as it should be."

– Mark Twain

"If you can't annoy somebody, there is little point in writing."

– Kingsley Amis

Atlanta AND THE
Southeast

"... first we have to read you your rights."

My friend formed a corporation, Analytical Systems, that would have branches to feed into the chipper that was this computer. It will help you if I tell you about my one and only friend who I met in Stamford. We remained friends until his untimely death.

Robert was the youngest member of the city council. He and I were introduced by my uncle. Robert was married and at that time had two rug rats who, when I first met them, were chasing each other across the backs of the sofa. The couple ended up with four children which brings memo to self. "Think carefully about really wanting a girl child." The four children are all boys, men now.

Robert was from Connecticut. We had the same values and became so close that we pledged that if anything happened to either one of us the other would step in to become a surrogate family member.

We found in New York, a lawyer who specialized in "penny stock" offerings. He had an associate who traveled the globe finding prospects. Had I known then . . . as the saying goes. What we had walked into was a Ponzi scheme. Their idea was to hype the offering to friends, family, and business associates and somehow keep the pigeons from selling the stock. If someone sold a sizable amount, more money had to be brought in to cover the withdrawal.

The brain trust shielded me from financial comings and goings. All I needed to do was sell, sell, sell. Sell market research and show up in New York for meetings. I remember the day the stock went public. The wife and I were on vacation. I was a nervous wreck until I got the call that it had been successful. I was suddenly a paper millionaire with a book full of gorgeous, in color, paper stock certificates. Unfortunately, the color wasn't green. But my mission remained the same, as did my knowledge about what was happening around me. So, how surprised was I when a certified letter commanded me to show up at the Securities and Exchange Commission (SEC) New York headquarters? Naïve as a babe, I went with no trepidation. Trepidation started after, "Hello."

I was in the new (now gone) World Trade Center Building, very high up. The view was stunning. After "hello," the agent said, "We have a few questions, but before we ask them, we have to Mirandize you." As many floors as we were up, were the number of floors my stomach dropped. The agent must have noticed the blood drain from all my exposed parts. He also must have realized he wasn't facing a schemer; he was facing a *schnook*. He told me that he and his partner didn't think I was liable; they merely wanted to fill in some spots in their investigation. What they were investigating, I still didn't know. I had to piece it together from the questions. Within months, our lawyer and his globe-trotting partner were cuffed, jailed, tried, and convicted. That's as close to jail as I ever want to get. That was my "enough is enough" moment. Now I needed to get a job. It turned out to be with the American Jewish Committee, the oldest human relations agency in the country. Coming up to its 75th anniversary, it had to that point totally escaped my attention. I had never heard of it.

Soon after, I could tell people that I had gotten my job through the NY Times, which I had. I made a call that was answered by a woman who sounded like Methusala's grandmother and that she had been smoking unfiltered cigarettes all her life. Her office was on the third floor of a building that looked worse than she did. After a brief interview, she made a call, and sent me to 165 E. 56th Street. There I was interviewed by three different people, all of whom were named Katz, and none of whom were related.

By the end of the day, I had been offered a job and a choice. Did I want to go to Houston, Texas, or Atlanta, GA? Houston reported to Dallas, which reported to the main frame. My work would be filtered through someone I had to make look good. I chose Atlanta. I had studied Atlanta in college, I had been there and loved it, and I liked my assignment which covered the deep South.

Here is an excerpt from my curriculum vitae that will give you a broad-brush peek at what I signed up for. It is solely a roadmap and not an ego trip. It is a small basket of issues but will give you the "why?" of some things I've already mentioned and will mention.

> "He has become well-known for his work with Catholic and Protestant Church leaders throughout the southeast, having coordinated interreligious dialogues with the Catholic Church, the Presbyterian Church (U.S.), the Southern Presbyterian Church, N.C. Baptist Association, and the Greek Orthodox Church. He also has founded three offshoots of the National Interreligious Task Force on Soviet Jewry and the international "Project Lifeline Letters." He was a board member of The Atlanta Interfaith Broadcasting Company in Atlanta. In 1986, Gralnick was asked by Edward A. McCarthy, Archbishop of Miami, to serve on the Catholic-Jewish Steering Committee for the September 11, 1987, Papal visit of Pope John Paul II. Tasks related to the visit involved security (working with city, county, state, and federal law enforcement agencies); invitation lists; program planning (which included a diplomatic reception the evening prior to the visit); and local protocol issues. Mr. Gralnick was paid the high honor of being introduced to the Pope.

Barry University President, Sr. Jeanne O'Laughlin, appointed Mr. Gralnick to the Advisory Board for the Department of Jewish Studies at this Catholic University."

●●●

Now the fun begins. What follows is a list of my states and some snarky, brief comments about them. Then we'll get down to the work done in their cities.

NORTH CAROLINA

The people are as nice as the state until that is you discuss politics.

SOUTH CAROLINA

The people are as nice as the state until that is you discuss politics . . .

TENNESSEE

Mountain folk who like distance between themselves and the next fellow.

GEORGIA

All those things you've read about Georgia . . . ? Yup

ALABAMA

Same deal . . .

MISSISSIPPI

. . . Not only true . . . But worse!

Every state had cities each of which provided different challenges not only for the AJC but for me.

Take a breath, take a snort, and get ready to march through the south.

First, we have to get there. It was the result of a transfer. Several things figured into it. One was demographics. Atlanta was a small (about 35,000) strong, united, wealthy Jewish community. It was still recovering from the bombing of the largest Reform synagogue in the city by the Klan. The hanging of Leo Frank, 'though many decades before, still hung over the community. Relatives on each side of the murder still lived in Atlanta. The relatives of Leo Frank wouldn't talk about it; the relatives of little Mary Phagan were stubborn in their feeling that Frank deserved what he got. What he got was being dragged out of jail and hanged before the trail. If you are not familiar with the story, you should be. The Leo Frank Story starring Jack Lemmon is about as good a look as you'll find. It is worth watching.

Off we went. Car packed with clothing, an infant, and two dogs, one of which was a 140 lb. Great Dane, we arrived, to paraphrase Johnny and June Carter Cash's line about Jackson, not in a fever but in a storm. With no GPS or cell phone to turn to when we were lost, I pulled into a K-mart shopping center to get more specific directions. The sky had that "Watch out!" look, signifying that the world might be coming to an end. It got very dark. The wind began to kick up. When my feet hit the cement, I had to lean forward to make headway. The problem was that the wind wasn't coming at me; it was swirling around me.

Suddenly, I was in a scene from Alice in Wonderland. All that was missing was the Mad Hatter. Trees began to bend over and wave their branches at me. Hats blown off people's heads were doing the Hora or other circle dances in the middle of the parking lot. Anything not cemented in place suddenly was imbued with life, each piece having a mind and direction of its own. The piece de resistance was the shopping carts. Like the broomlets in The Sorcerer's Apprentice, they began moving around. Some seemed to have a leader and followed it; some were just doing their own thing. Finally, a voice cut through the air. "Hey, you! Get the hell inside. There's a tornado a-comin'!" Oh.

I hustled the family out of the car and ran inside. It wasn't a direct hit where I was, but that night, safe in the motel, we saw on television where it was a direct hit, that the Corinthian columns had been stripped off the Governor's mansion, that the tornado smashed the central mail station like a giant foot had stomped on its roof. There was a locomotive that had been tossed a few hundred yards through the air like a toy. A news reporter interviewed a woman who had an out-of-body, but fortunately not an out-of-car, experience. The tornado took her for a ride, many feet above the ground, and then dropped her. It was just a peachy experience. Described as a roaring freight train by some, I don't think that was her opinion.

Such was our welcome to Georgia, a place where one didn't listen to weather forecasts at one's peril.

Tornado: Described as a roaring freight train.

Sometimes there are practical reasons for a move. One was that my predecessor was Orthodox, leading an organization that was certainly not. Another was that the Israeli Consulate was also in Atlanta. I had the kind of experience that would make me a good man for dealing with diplomacy. Finally, a long-time secretary in the office needed to go. Everybody agreed, but not one person had the "you know whats" to do it. National decided that sending in a new boss was the best way. My first official act was putting someone on the unemployment rolls and taking someone off them when I hired my choice for secretary. After about two weeks of working with her, the firing became easy. The nearly nine years in Atlanta were a career in themselves as you'll see.

The other reason was to put some life into our non-office chapters in those states. As were the states different one from the other so were the leaders of the chapters in those states. I had several large categories of things to do; I had to become known to my membership, the media, and the interfaith community. The latter was because Jews were two-tenths of one percent of the Georgia population. My members wanted us to interact with the world around us. There was, however, a lot more to interfaith work. The state is primarily Evangelical and Baptist; hardcore Southern Methodists made up almost all the rest. Catholics were a mere .5% of the state's population. Atlanta being the home of the King family, one particular black church, Ebenezer Baptist Church, was extremely important but so was the array of other black denominations and the nuances that separated them. It was like going back to school.

Then there were all those white denominations. Here's an example. There are Baptists, Foot-washing Baptists and multiple other kinds of Baptists. Presbyterians came in Southern and Northern denominations. So did the Methodists. And the Church of Christ Scientist? I don't quite know where that fits in.

It was one thing to pull out my comparative religions text from college. It was totally another thing to meet the people, hear about their religion from them, and sometimes watch it practiced. Talking in tongues, snake worship, foot-washing, and learning the Apostolic Creed became critical to my job. That is if I wanted people to know I had taken the time to study, and cared enough to learn, about their faith. My Spanish professor once said, "There is no better feeling than to be able to talk to a person in their own language." There is a parallel about knowing a person's religion. However, the key to this section is how I will tell you about it without losing you.

Atlanta, however, was my main gig. We had a storied chapter, and here come the stories followed by those from other cities in other states.

We'll start with the learning experience that was my introduction to the AJC membership. I would be the keynote speaker at a member's luncheon.

We lived in the suburbs near the Cumberland Mall. Each morning I commuted to work with the radio as my companion. My brother was still working at CBS, so I listened to CBS News on the car's radio. Every so often, the raconteur, Charles Osgood, famous for his humor often done in rhyme, presented something. This one was about work. It struck me very funny. I was giggling in the car to no one. "Wow!" I said to me, "that would go great in my speech!" It didn't. The key to public speaking is, "know thy audience." I didn't know this one. This one didn't care that it was my maiden voyage. They had their own stories to share—cards, kids, sports teams—and share them they did. 'made no never mind,' as is said in Georgia, that I was speaking. So much for Southern hospitality. From the audience I faced, which filled the room, rose a din of crisscrossing conversations, punctuated by silverware banging on plates, cups clinking against saucers, chairs scraping the floor as they moved in and out from the table. I soldiered on. I spoke too long, and with the help of Charles Osgood, I spoke even longer.

I wish I still had the Osgood piece to show you I wasn't totally out of my mind. It was funny—promise. I finished. There greeted me a smattering of applause, and the audience dissipated. I had been driven to the event by the chairman of our board, my mentor (here's an example of his Deep South wisdom: "Don't say anything about anyone that you wouldn't say to their face because you're probably talking to their cousin!"). At the end, he grabbed my elbow and whisked me out of the room. Looking at me dead in the eye, he had this appraisal: "Don't ever do that again." Lesson learned.

There was another memorable country club event. We were honoring our oldest member who was in the first graduating class at Harvard Law. At 90-something, he did 100 push-ups every morning. He also felt the rules of etiquette no longer applied. No woman's fanny was safe if it passed by his hand. The award was presented; he stood to give his thank you speech. Without a thought or afterthought, his address was full of stories that included the words darkies, coloreds, and nigras. The wait staff dressed in white and was entirely black. After a few minutes and a few "nigras," one of the waiters dropped a plate. It hit the floor with a resounding crash and shattered into pieces. At "coloreds," another waiter did the same. The honoree's entire speech was punctuated with trays, plates, and glasses dropping and smashing. It was like listening to the finale of the 1812 Overture. That was the last award given to him.

Other happenings weren't funny at all. The Southern Baptist Convention announced that God didn't listen to the prayers of Jews. This started a long round of meetings, some individual, some in groups. It is one thing for someone to think that belief in Jesus' divinity is necessary for salvation. It is another to have it publicly stated by the country's largest Protestant denomination. We had some allies. Billy Graham disagreed. Jerry Falwell grudgingly called it overstated.

There were individual heroes. One was the man who held the interfaith portfolio for the convention whose job it was to meet, befriend, and convert people. He had deep, abiding issues with the convention's work with other faiths. He expressed these feelings in a trifold publication that presented a new etiquette for missionizing the Jews. Demonization was his thanks. He wasn't fired. It was worse than being fired; he was exiled. He lost his title and was appointed pastor of a small SBC (Southern Baptist Convention) church in the land of Congregational faith, northern New England. He died a disillusioned man, even though we, his fellow supporters, stayed in touch, and provided him meaningful things to do to express his belief that God loved all His people and therefore heard all their prayers.

Let's take a break for a personal story. It's a dog story. I've always been a dog person. In both previous books, you would have learned that. This is a Stamford-Atlanta story. It ends in Atlanta, so I'll put it here. We lived in a suburb of Stamford called Ridgefield. Our house was on a wooded lot that was joined by another lot through which ran a brook. The street was named Silver Brook Lane. Woodland surrounded three sides of the house which was two stories high. The plus was a large two-room basement. There was certainly enough room for a dog. Not only did I want one for me, but I thought, given the property's isolation, having one to protect the family would be a good idea.

I've always loved Great Danes. I had one in college that saved my life when a house fire broke out. A Dane would be the perfect fit for what I needed. We found a harlequin pup and ingeniously (maybe not so much . . .) came up with the name Patches. If well-bred, Danes are naturally protective but use their size and weight in passive-aggressive ways. If someone comes to the door, the Dane likely will position itself between the visitor and family. If the dog gets the ok from its owner or even a sense that all is well, it moves. If not—it doesn't. Being foolish enough to try and push by gets you met with a growl that seems to emanate from the bowels of the earth. It is a rich, deep sound. It usually suffices to stop the person in their tracks.

There can be an aggressive side.

Remember when one bought gas and signed the credit card receipt? An attendant handed a plastic tray holding the charge slip through the window for signature. If the baby was in the car, that was not permitted. Not by me, mind you, but by Patches.

We had guests. My wife was very pregnant. The dog seemed to be particularly watchful. We had friends over, the city councilman, Robert, from Stamford and his wife. There was candy on the lamp-stand near my wife's left hand. To get it, he had to stand up and lean over her. Also, not permissible. The dog bolted upright from what appeared to have been a sound sleep and, in a nano-second, she was nose to chest with my friend. That was followed by his re-seating himself and asking meekly, "Would you please pass the candy?"

She loved to play. Chasing a ball was heaven. Taking a tennis ball from that huge, wet mouth was short of heaven. On occasion, she would go into the woods and return, proud as punch, with a branch often as long as she was. She stood five foot ten inches. Watching her maneuver something that long, often 2-3" around, through the brush was a sight. She'd drop it at my feet and act like she'd brought me the best gift money could buy.

We'd just as soon have left a child when we moved than to have left a dog. She took up two people's space, so she rode in the back of the station wagon.

We lived at the end of a cul-de-sac. A three-tier wood fence separated the street from a cow pasture. Patches would lay out in the middle of the street's bowl, sun herself and watch the children. She adopted all of them around the bowl. Up the block was out of her jurisdiction. One of the things she eyed was the cows. One day, the perfect storm of child protection arose in her mind. The cows came down from the pasture towards the fence while my son ran toward them. The dog jumped up, cut off my son, wheeled around, and cleared the fence in three bounds. Having done that, she cleared the cows. It was amazing to watch.

Our second son was born in Atlanta. I had trepidations about how the dog would react to the newcomer. After all, she weighed over 140 lbs. and could carry tree branches in her mouth. As a teething puppy, she had chewed the arm off the couch—all the way down to the frame. Trusting my judgment, I laid the baby on the rug, sat next to him, and called over the dog, motioning her to lie down. First, she sniffed the baby a few times, then lay down, putting her head on the baby's belly as if to say, "Ok, this one's mine, too."

Our next-door neighbor had a son the age of my oldest. He was a sneaky kid with a nasty streak. One day I saw him poke Patches in the ribs with a pointy stick. She winced. I called him over and said, "Tony, if I were you, I'd stay away from her. You just lost her friendship." Sure enough, the next time he tried to come into our house, a menacing growl told him, "You're not welcome here."

Here's another intrusion of life. On the other side of us was the Executive Chef of the Atlanta Hilton, mentioned later in the Kiaweh Island meetings. He'd put out a Fourth of July spread on the street that would have been easily $75 a person. It was free. His house was dead center in the bowl of the road. His lawn ran down to meet the glass front of his house. Mother had taken son shopping. She pulled into our driveway and did something one should never do. She left the kid in the car, thinking that the car seat would be safe enough. It wasn't. A few years later, the car company informed us that our car had a safety defect. Left on an incline, which our driveway was, the gears might slip, and guided by no one, the car would begin moving. As for slipping, my son slipped out of the car seat and crawled up front to see where mom was. He knocked into the gear shift. As mom returned to the car, she watched this.

Like an overly large toy car guided electronically by an unseen controller, the car moved down the driveway. When it hit the street, the street's curvature made it swing around so it faced the chef's house. At this point, two things happened. The car started forward, and my son jumped out. The car, seemingly on a mission, headed for the house. It hit and jumped the curb, nosed into the depression on the lawn, and didn't stop until its front had pushed about two feet into the neighbor's living room. Unfortunately, in that two-foot space was a display case that held Mrs. Chef's Lalique collection, which was now mostly porcelain dust. Our relationship was never quite the same.

So, as we came to the end of the street, we come to this story's end. When having our house built, we converted the garage into a playroom for the kids and a bedroom for Patches. She had repeatedly earned her keep. Another example came with winter. Atlanta is prone to freezing temperatures and nasty ice storms. One day, the ice brought down the power lines, and we had no electricity, meaning no heat. We did have a fireplace in which I built a roaring fire. But the house was cold as night fell. I tacked two blankets over the passageways at both ends of the living room. That would seal in the heat. The time came to put the kids down. Patches lay down in front of the fireplace, and the boys slept tucked up against her belly.

Early one morning, they burst into our bedroom. We had taught both kids that if they got up earlier than we did to play in the playroom, so this was unusual. "We can't wake up Patches! We can't wake up Patches!" The night before, she had eaten her dinner but just didn't seem herself. Dogs with deep chests are prone to something called bloat. It's when gas builds up, and the intestines flip, trapping the gas. Unless surgery is performed immediately, it is almost always fatal. Patches was dead.

I was about to learn the meaning of "dead weight." It was raining cats and dogs. Thunder was booming. Lightning was flashing. I was hysterical, crying. I had to lift her to put her in the back of the wagon. Within seconds we were both soaked to the skin. She felt like she weighed 340 lbs., not 140. I don't know how I got to the vet between the rain and the tears. I jumped out of the car into the teeming rain, ran up the stairs, and was met by a sign, "Gone for the day—Florida-Georgia game." I had many reasons to curse the South. Now I had another. I began pounding on the door. Finally, an attendant opened it. I took her front, he her back. I wept harder on the way home than it was raining . . . We'd lost a family member. Amen.

Harlequin Great Dane—That's a lotta lovin'!

Georgia

MACON – ATHENS

Small cities with lots of small minds.

We've established that religion is a big deal in Georgia. Here are two more examples to underscore it. I got a call from a rabbi in Macon, Ga. One of his congregants was an insurance broker. His largest account was the school district. The administration decided that in the high school his son attended, each homeroom class would start with a prayer in the name of Jesus. When his son objected, his teacher told him he could stand in the hall during the prayer. The rabbi wanted me to investigate the situation. I spoke to the father; he backed his son. He would not let his son be isolated in the hall, made out to be a heathen outcast. If the District wouldn't intercede, then he would sue. The higher-ups came to him and suggested that if he wanted his contract with the district renewed, he might want to re-think the suit. He wouldn't and didn't. The decision almost bankrupted him. Anti-Semitic calls, signs, and graffiti came in a deluge with, finally, the loss of the contract. He had to relent to save his family. Score another one for Jesus.

After this bru-ha-ha, the rabbi suggested we come down and hold a community meeting on what the constitution and the law said about the separation of church and state. I had a young, articulate, and very intelligent assistant director. Her husband was a lawyer. Together they prepared a presentation, and she asked me to let her present it. I agreed but said I would be going with her. I wasn't afraid she'd misstate something; I was afraid for her safety. In the middle of her speech, a little old lady (I'm being literal here) bolted out of her seat. Armed with an umbrella held like a jousting pole, she charged the podium screaming, "Heathen! Heathen! You're the devil's spawn." That was it for the meeting: Jesus two, constitution zero.

Yet sometimes, a breath of fresh air is to be found in such places, and it can be found on the hottest and most humid of days. The Klan decided to take advantage of the situation and announced a march in Macon. I went to the chief of police. He patted me on the shoulder and said I shouldn't worry; he had things in hand. The chief

Jesus

decided he didn't want to deny a permit. That would give the Klan what it wanted, publicity. He set the march to begin at the bottom of the steepest street in town, going from bottom to top. It was a brutal summer's day. Klan robes then were heavy. Many of the faithful decided not to show up. Fewer than a dozen robed men nearing heat stroke made their way up the hill and out of town. Score one for the good guys.

It is said that the only thing wrong with Atlanta is that it is surrounded by Georgia. On a trip up to The University of Georgia in Athens, I stopped at a gas station where I got a taste of that. A black family with their children followed me in. Fresh out of a farm catalog, replete with overhauls, they were met with a growl: "Hold on there, folks, we don't serve no niggers here." I thought it might cost me my life to say something, so I didn't. Besides, I was so shocked nothing would come out of my mouth.

These attitudes were not only of the unwashed. One of my board members, who was filthy rich and lived in a sprawling Atlanta mansion, decided he wanted to introduce me to an equally rich potential donor. He told me to bring my sales stuff. He drove. I threw my stuff in the back. When we arrived, I reached into the back for my briefcase. He scolded me. "Where are you taking that thing?" I told him I had my notes and handouts in it. His reply was: "Only uppity niggers carry briefcases. Leave it in the car." Oh.

Time for a Break

Sometimes its better to deal with the stress—and stay home.

Everyone needs a vacation. Having now two children and three dogs (Patches hadn't yet passed. We also had a Scottish Terrier and a Dachshund—don't ask . . .) and living in this twilight zone of the world, I needed one. A great thing about Atlanta is that it is easy to reach two sets of mountains, North Georgia and South Georgia, plus the beaches of Savannah. My wife was a sun worshipper, so we chose the beach and embarked on "the vacation from hell."

We didn't know where to go and didn't have much spendable income, so I asked a minister with whom I had become friends. He knew just the place. It was right on the beach; he and his wife had stayed there. Later, thinking back on things, I should have picked up on the cultural differences. Jackie Mason in his routine about the differences between Jews and Gentiles, says you go into a Jewish home, and everything is covered in plastic. You first get a tour of the paintings, silverware, and anything else of value. Gentiles, he said, are never settled. They're always "hopping and klopping" (moving around, nailing this to that). "The living room is becoming the dining room, the dining room will be a library, the toilet has to go someplace else." Well, that was a fair description of the state of my friend's house. But I missed the obvious and took the motel phone number. I made reservations. On the appointed date, we set out for Savannah.

Atlanta to Savannah is now an easy drive with the interstate built. Then it was state and county roads and usually took six hours if the traffic was in your favor. How could we have anticipated what was to come? I kid you not that from the moment the car door closed behind us, my son began to cry. Let's replace cry. He was wailing, screaming, and thrashing around. Did he have a fever? No. Was a diaper pin (you read that correctly) sticking to him? No. Was it the car seat? Not that either. He was inconsolable. After about two hours, we stopped at a restaurant. The decibel level of his shrieking had people looking at us, but not because they were disturbed. They were the kinds of looks that said, "I think we better call the police." We left. He cried for the next four hours.

Blessedly, we arrived before I either murdered him or committed suicide, the odds of either having increased because the motel complex either had no numbers or the numbers were in places you couldn't see from the car. The caterwauling continued and I couldn't find the bloody place. Did I mention the summer heat? The humidity? The lack of automobile air-conditioning? Finally, I found our part of the place, and unpacked the car. We were on the second floor—where it is hotter in the summer than on the first floor. I couldn't wait to swing open the door to paradise. Again, I should have known. Paradise doesn't come at the price we were paying. This is what faced us.

A long, incredibly weathered, two-story building on stilts was our vacation home. A long, creaky, wooden staircase was our staircase to heaven—dogs, child, suitcases had to go up it. Oh yes, the very pregnant wife too. It opened into our room. Getting settled meant several trips up and down, one carrying the kid. I arrived, dripping wet and soaked through my clothing from sweat, to face a scowling wife who informed me that the unit had no air- conditioning. My dear friend, rapidly losing his place in the friendship pantheon, had neglected that detail. It was hot and muggy. One advantage was if the children wanted to play in the sand, they didn't have to be schlepped down to the beach. Plenty of sand was on the floor—along with sand fleas and black flies. The flies were so big that one wouldn't need Clydesdales if the flies were hitched up to a wagon. And how much cheaper to feed they would be! The best I can tell you is that there was no crying on the way home.

This not being one of the highlights of my stay in Georgia, let's move on to something that was.

NEXT UP:

Ebenezer Baptist Church

It didn't look important but oh how important it was.

After Dr. King died, the world-famous Ebenezer Baptist Church fell on hard times. The board decided it needed an executive director. They asked me to join the search committee. I did and then became a confidant/advisor to the newly hired professional. Ebenezer was no architectural wonder, nor was it in a great neighborhood. For those of you who believe history can speak, that's what Ebenezer did. There was a certain something about it, whether empty or full, that one just felt. I felt it. And I felt it more when asked to be a guest speaker from the pulpit on a commemoration day.

I had already spoken from my fair share of pulpits, but not this one. This was different. To stand where Martin stood. For a white man, especially a young white man, to craft a message for a black audience is a major undertaking. So deeply meaningful emotionally, so immensely historical, I fear I've failed you by putting it into words. Add the fact that this congregation regularly heard powerful sermons from great preachers that rang loud, clear, and profound. I was nervous. I would become more anxious when they announced the order of speakers. I was to follow Ebenezer's first legend, Daddy King.

Daddy King was an old-time preacher. Not one who believed that fashion had much to do with messages of salvation, he had a rumpled look about him. As this revered man made his way to the podium, age and sadness weighing on him, I didn't know what to expect. He got to the platform, eschewing the help of several staff members. He didn't stand behind it. He stood alongside it. After a few words, it became apparent he didn't need any amplification for his voice to penetrate every nook, cranny, and corner of the place. He stood alongside the podium because he didn't want it to separate him from his flock. The nonchalant way he threw his left arm over the top of the pulpit, his hand hanging over the top, struck me as a posture one might use among friends. Listening to him was like listening to a powerful motor warming up. He waved to a few people, he'd "and how are you's" to some others. He was doing his own warm-up act.

Truthfully, I don't remember what he said, only how he said it. His words began as a low rumble, almost like he was speaking that way to make people lean in to hear him. Within a few minutes, he had everyone in the palm of his vocal cords. Then the volume began to rachet up. Every few sentences he boomed out had the same rumble. After five or six minutes, I could see this old man may have lost a step or two, but he still was a master of the spoken word. He spoke for about 25 minutes, the last 10 or 12 of which were so rousing that the audience was with him and into it. Calls from them urged him on. When he was finished, he was spent but so were his listeners. There would be a short break, and I would be up next. I began to shiver.

I am almost unknown by those I was about to face, and I was following a legend with the vocal power of a cannon. This would surely be a test of my mettle. And you know what? I did fine. I was a student of leaders who gave great speeches, whether I liked them or not—Hitler, Castro, de Gaulle, and MLK. I had always been fascinated by the black preacher's particular style, which started slowly and built to a crescendo. It was a style taught in seminary that moved people from the backs of their seats to the fronts and sometimes to a standing position. I had woven together a speech that spoke to the things we had in common, saying slavery was slavery, whether it was 100 years ago or thousands of years ago that as former slaves, Jews were taught to fight for the human condition and against those who chose to make it worse. My speed increased, my voice got louder, and by the end, I was exhausted. By George, or by MLK, they liked it. I was shaking like a leaf by the time I left the podium. My legs were Jello. My hands were shaking like I had a palsy. It took me three days to recover, but I just had the experience of a lifetime—and maybe done some good.

WILLIAM A. GRALNICK

Moving On

When one's career is young, it is more fun to go rather than stay.

There were light moments and odd moments. Atlanta in the '70s had two major Jewish institutions. One was Reform. It was known as "The Temple," and had one of the most universally admired Reform rabbis in the country, Rabbi Richard Marx. The other, the Conservative Synagogue, was Ahavath Achim, known for obvious reasons as AA. The first was German-Jewish-based. It was the one bombed by the KKK not twenty years before I arrived. The other's base was Russian-Jewish. It, too, had a towering rabbinic figure, Rabbi Harry Epstein. He held that pulpit for over forty years—and it was not his first pulpit.

I joined The Temple mostly because my leadership was its leadership and because its program goals were similar to AJC's, which also historically had a German-Jewish base. The Temple had a new, young southern Rabbi who had been a salesman. How did he come to the pulpit? One day on his sales rounds, he had a religious experience and decided he wanted to become a rabbi. Alvin Sugarman became known over the years as "the" rabbi to see when politicians or church leaders wanted to have contact with Jewish leadership. He hired for his assistant a bright-eyed young man fresh out of seminary. Ed Cohen was his name, and his brand of Judaism was pitched to things of this day, not those past days in Jewish life. I was in attendance one Friday night when this happened.

It was Rabbi Cohen's first sermon. As was the tradition at The Temple, at the end of services, he stood at the door, as do Christian ministers, to greet the congregation as it exited. An older woman, taken by his sermon and fresh face, came up to him and said, "Rabbi,

I attend AA, but I want you to know how inspiring I found you." His response? "I'm so sorry for your addiction and applaud you for your work in beating it." Truth. She looked non-plussed. At a break in the action, I whispered in his ear, "Rabbi around here, AA is a synagogue, not an addiction program." Now he was the one with the non-plussed look on his face.

Richard Warren Sears—notice, no green-checked suit.

Then there was the story of the green and white-checked suit. I was a big boy now and buying my own clothing. Early into my years in Atlanta, I saw a suit that caught my eye. The large green and white-checked pattern was a stand-out. I bought it. Thinking back on it, I'd say it resembled a green and white chessboard. It was much more inner-city New York than downtown Atlanta, but I loved it. I felt people could see me comin'. In the Atlanta Jewish community, that was a no-no.

I had some very influential board members. One was an heir to the Sears and Roebuck fortune, though I forget now whether it was Sears or Roebuck to which her genes belonged. Her husband was as Deep South as one could be, a white shoe lawyer with a drawl who was so prim and proper I thought he was a little "fay," as the term was back then. When he would excuse himself from a meeting to go to the bathroom, he'd say he had to go "Tee-Tee." Gee willikers.

They graciously opened their luxurious home for me to speak to the membership. I recall my reaction when the sliding glass doors in the living room opened to the patio and pool area. The space looked like it was the size of a football field. The party was a throwback to 1940's movies, but not intentionally. Everything had to be perfect, and it was. To be sure, I was too. I received a call the day before, and an unmistakable drawl said, "You know that new suit you just bought? The green and white one? I began to beam, sure that a compliment was coming. He continued, "Don't wear it, not in my home or anywhere else I might be." Yikes. I chose a blue suit and white shirt, button-down of course, and didn't use the style of speech I had used at Ebenezer.

Hilton Without Paris

I previously mentioned Kiawah Island, SC. It was rumored to have restrictive covenants against Jews and others. The hotel was managed by the Hilton Management crew. Jewish communities were in an uproar. They looked for an Achilles heel. AJC found it back in Atlanta where Hilton was planning to break ground on what would be the crown jewel in their hospitality tiara. First, there were legal actions against the restrictions. As is often the case, this was a David and Goliath exercise. Hilton had more lawyers than we had personnel of any kind. And they were good. Hilton paid them exceptionally well to win. Yet, just as Achilles learned, even the best armor has its chink. It might take years, but the law was on our side. But there was a more significant chink that became Hilton's Achilles' heel. They had begun the advertising and marketing for the jewel in the Hilton Hotel crown, a hotel with a revolving roof-top restaurant. There would be a several-story gap between the last floor of rooms and the Russian tea-room type very high-end restaurant and lounge on the top. The first time one took that elevator ride would be heart-stopping. For a momentary flash, you were in a space capsule with no building to cradle you. The first time I did it, I spent some time in the bar before sitting down and eating, otherwise I wouldn't have been able to hold a fork.

I learned that before a major property opened, the marketing department was supposed to sell, in this case, over one million pre-opening room and conference rentals. They got going immediately. Then came our monkey wrench. AJC got together a cross-section of powerful Jewish business leadership and requested a meeting with the VP of marketing. Were the rules in Kiawah not changed,

The shovel that builds riches.

Atlanta's Jewish community would lead a boycott against this hotel. We got their attention. We got the meeting, a great lunch, and a very courteously presented brush-off.

I called the next day, having taken the lead for the community on the issue. "We aren't going away," was my message. Next came a meeting between the International Vice President of Hilton and me. His card was a unique message, subliminally suggesting power. On the front was what you'd expect. On the back, it simply said, "Millionaire." In the mid-'70s that was still a big deal, especially when you flew in on a private jet. This time I was nervous as a cat. Before lunch, he introduced me to the executive team, the GM of the hotel, the Executive Chef (who, as you learned was my next door neighbor), and the department heads. We talked turkey while we ate caviar. My position was simple, and I tried to present it simply. Hilton was suborning antisemitism. We would fight that regardless of who the actors were. Hilton was the only one with a dog in the fight, and it was a fabulously expensive dog at that. Not only wouldn't I budge, but I also couldn't since I was speaking for the Jewish community. I seemed to have made progress, and he graciously asked if he couldn't accompany me to my car. Unfortunately, I was so nervous I forgot where the car was. It was an enormous garage. After minutes of fruitless searching, he called for a golf cart and driver. In total mortification, I was driven up and down every level. At least, I remembered what kind of car I drove. We found it. Also, graciously, he never again mentioned it.

There was to be one more meeting. It was with Baron Hilton. He was the *capo di tutti capos*. Regrettably, Paris was too young to be in attendance . . . Again, with the lunch, again, with the power introductions, again, being treated like I had something over them, and they knew they had to fix it. Mr. Hilton came up with a proposition. It would require trust on both sides. He said I would have to give him some time. He couldn't just close the Kiawah Island contract, nor did he want to "fire" the Saudis, which would cause an international incident and potentially hurt Hilton's projects and products around the globe. Give him some time, and he would see to the end of it. On my side, there would be no gaudy press releases and press conferences about how the American Jewish Committee and Atlanta's Jewish community rubbed Hilton's nose in it. I could assure the smallest group of my most trusted leaders that a deal had been done. We would stop talking of a boycott; they would publicly state their abhorrence of antisemitism and prejudice of any type. Considering that this hotel was in Georgia, that was a powerful statement.

I never knew how they dealt with their end of the problem. There was news in the South Carolina press. When the contract ended, Hilton didn't renew it. I did get a lot of appreciation. I received an invitation to the ground-breaking. I still have the toolbox-size (fake) gold-inscribed shovel. For my wedding anniversary, Hilton treated us to a suite and dinner in the spaceship. Whenever I had to impress someone, including family and friends, I had a number to call. The caviar and all the helpings would be on the house. *Chazor* is a Yiddish word that means one who takes more than is polite. It usually means eating everything reachable on the holiday table. It also means taking advantage of an offer more than one should. I had become mature enough not to be a *chazor*. In my nine years in Atlanta, I only called the number once. That was the right thing to do for the reputation of Atlanta's Jewish community. For me, other duties called.

●●●

To give you an idea of how taxing the job was, I subscribed to six newspapers to keep up with my territory. I developed a routine. I'd pull out every section that had nothing to do with local news and culture. They went into the trash; recycling hadn't become a thing yet. Then I'd set aside a few hours a week to read what was left. It was laborious but served me well. I could fly in from Atlanta and talk "local" to my very impressed members. I also had a basis for suggesting programs and finding existing programs that involved AJC.

Stop Thief!

You can't stop who you don't see.

A work-life balance is essential. One must take time out for family which I now had. I had a two-year-old and one that had just arrived. It took a year or so to get settled personally and professionally. I saw an ad for a spectacular amusement park called Six Flags Georgia. Even though it was not in Atlanta, and I had no idea what the flags represented, I decided to take the family on the two-hour jaunt to get there and make a day of it. The day started badly and then got worse. Sometimes, an angel alights on your shoulder to straighten it all out. Mine arrived just in time.

There was a huge traffic backup going to the park. A kid in a sports car was racing toward the jam and forgot to stop. Then came the screeching of tires and the sound of metal twisting into artistic shapes. I told my wife to take the kids and stand in the shade while I went to offer badly needed help. The European sports car had its emergency brake between the driver and the driver's console. Part of the brake ripped open his leg down to the bone, which I could see. I don't recommend the experience. I tended to him with first aid, talking to him calmly, and was much relieved when the EMTs arrived.

We got into our car, me evincing hero-like composure, finished the trip, parked, and soon we were ready for our day of fun and sun. I reached for my wallet, which, when driving long distances, I tucked into a space under the dash. It wasn't there. Could I have forgotten it? No, because we had stopped on the way, and I had used it. In the file of "no good deed goes unpunished," add that while I was rendering first aid, some scoundrel rendered me wallet-less.

Now, my family and I are at the ticket booth with no money. I blurted out my story. I even showed her the blood that had gotten on my clothes. It was here the angel swooped in and handed me a free family pass. Praise the Lord.

So that was something someone else did to me. This next story is something that I did to me. My job was to develop bright ideas and implement them. My average at work for doing that was high. At home, not always. We lived about 25 miles from downtown. One could use the highway or the suburban streets to get there. Either way, it was rush hour, took a lot of time, and used a lot of gas. "Buy a moped" was my solution to what wasn't that much of a problem. It was inexpensive, cute, easy to handle, and used about a tablespoon of gas for endless miles. Proud I was to be such a smart consumer. Then came the first meeting downtown.

There Oughta Be a Law

OH? THERE WAS ONE?

God is generally kind. (S)He gives hints. His (Her) assumption is that you'll pick up on them. Like the ancient Israelites, I didn't. My hint came the day I brought home my new purchase. I did a few dry runs up and down the street. All went well. My wife thought it was the cutest thing since teddy bears and wanted to hop on. I offered a tutorial, but she wasn't the tutorial type. "How hard can this be? It's like a toy!" With no idea of what made it go or, more importantly, stop, she jumped on the already running moped. It took off across the street like a horse that had been slapped.

God can be kind even if you're stupid. Devine intervention is all that can account for the fact that she fell off just before her head hit a fire hydrant. Not wearing a helmet, she came within millimeters of a fractured skull or death. That was God's hint that I should return the adorable little thing that was Chucky in another form. But I didn't and came the day for the first, and I might add only ride to a meeting during which I learned it's best to listen to God and the legislature and wear a helmet.

In Atlanta, men wore suits and ties to meetings. Some judges insisted that lawyers wear only white, starched shirts—no blues, yellows, or stripes—in court. Plain white button-downs or don't show up. Ties were *de riguer*. While summer in Atlanta isn't long, like in Florida, it is hot. My first realization that this moped adventure was a bad idea came when I left the neighborhood and set out on one of the major arteries. The heat from the street, the heat from the exhaust pipes, the heat beating down from the sky and back up from the concrete—in minutes, rivulets of sweat were coursing down my back. Minutes more, and I had sweated through my shirt. My suit jacket acted as a barrier against atmospheric exchange. All my body heat, and all that other heat, was held close by my suit jacket. I was poached. The helmet acted as a pressure cooker and began boiling my brain. Sweat was running down my forehead into my eyes making sight a challenge. They burned. Tears were rolling down my face. Not a good thing in traffic.

Aside from being hot, it was scary. I didn't realize how small the moped was and how big the cars whizzing by me were. A minor mistake by a car's driver or made by me would mean the hospital.

There were also oddities about a moped of which its driver had to be aware—something about the fuel injection, shifting gears, and the probability that the moped would stall. I didn't know that stuff because I don't read manuals; I should have read this one. The moped sputtered, coughed, and stopped. People trying to get to work in the morning at drive time are not nice. I de-moped'ed and wrangled it through several lanes of traffic onto the sidewalk to see what was what. Under my soaked shirt's wrist was floating my watch. I began to wonder if the warranty covered a surfeit of sweat. The watch told me I had too many minutes left in my ride to be on time, that is, if I got it restarted.

I could go on. I won't. Let's end this saga with an image. An imposing skyscraper with an enormous, immaculate, shiny lobby. Security guards were the receptionists. Out of place in it was a young person in a suit who looked like he had been pulled out of a 19th-century clothes-washing vat, so wet that when he walked, his feet made squishing sounds—that was me. A ride up to the top and entry into a long conference room with an equally long, waxed-to-perfection wooden conference table brought me face to face with a dozen men dressed, you got it, in suits, white button-down shirts, and ties. One said, "Good God, man! What happened to you?"

I sold the moped.

Terror!

●●●

THEN CAME THE CHILD MURDERS
AND MORE

Before Sandy Hook, before Columbine, before the University of Texas, and before Pulse or even thoughts of such happenings came the Atlanta child murders. It began, oddly enough, with the murder of two black adults. Then black children disappeared. Everyone, black and white, thought it must be the Klan. If people could reason during such events, they would have known it couldn't have been the Klan. Not great organizers or planners, the perpetrators would have been seen or left clues. The killer had to be a lone wolf. Yet, when a child care facility blew up, that sealed the deal. After all, hadn't the Klan bombed The Temple just across town, not twenty years before? It seemed an eternity until the police announced that a faulty gas line caused the explosion. Few believed that.

As the disappearances continued to occur and bodies continued to be found, the tension in the city began to rise. Everyone had a theory. Everyone had a criticism. Everyone who had a child, white or black, was terrified. Even kids knew. My wife and I were going out to a movie. We hired a babysitter for our five-year-old. As we closed the screen door behind us, our son put both hands on it and asked plaintively, "Is the bad man going to get me?" You can't imagine the ice water that replaces your blood when faced with such a question.

And it must be answered with more than a "no." We returned for hugs, kisses, and assurances that we would lock the doors and he would be safe. We probably should have stayed. It was a rotten, nerve-racking two hours. We were as glad to be home as he was to have us home.

The police were on twelve-hour shifts, days off canceled. There were more different kinds of law enforcement agencies and task forces in town than you could count. A car's backfire would turn people into stone. Unrecognized noises at home were the cause for breaking out in a sweat. Shotguns were at hand once the sun went down.

Aside from experiencing this as a parent, I was a professional whose agency dealt with such things. I had two more bites at this awful apple. Atlanta didn't have enough cops, and they all were exhausted from work and tension. And there were no clues—hundreds of tips, but none that produced anything. I had a brainstorm. Why not train civilians to do desk jobs? It could free up cops from inside offices to be outside on the streets. The chief liked it. My board liked it. Everyone except some cops who had to leave cushy desk jobs liked it. The program, which required trainers and social workers, gave me the feeling that I had done something meaningful and important. That's a good feeling.

Then came the second bite. It was bitter. The United States Department of Justice Community Relations Task Force came to help. I don't remember how the director came to me, but he did. The idea was to create mixed task forces of people with different skills, including citizen volunteers. Every night after sundown, a group headed out into parts of town that could easily hide a kidnapped child or its body. Yes, we had cops with us. No, that didn't calm us in the least. I remembered the radio program "The Shadow," where the announcer would intone, "Who knows what evil lies in the hearts of man?" We were finding out.

Motel 6 is better—much.

●●●

Children continued to disappear. There were innumerable numbers of leads to track down. Total gone—29. Finally a young Black man named Wayne Williams was arrested but for the murders of the two black men! He rests in prison today, denying his guilt and also being denied pardons. Yet, from the day of his arrest there were no more murders. Go figure. Alfred Hitchock? Still a mystery based on a conviction resting on circumstantial evidence. Still . . . no more murders.

I'm here to tell you to stay home after midnight or certainly don't be out alone no matter where you live. Weird people do weird things after midnight. It's a running joke between my wife of 33 years and me that she likes to be home when the clock strikes nine. After my experience on this task force, I'm happy to watch the clock. What did we find? First, let me say that tromping through high brush, wild sticker bushes, and tripping over trash was unpleasant. Every stumble in the night heightened the tension. We had flashlights, but we couldn't see much of anything until we were on top of it. We found:

- piles of trash and human waste. Searching it was part of the gig.
- dead dogs, cats, and skeletons of things that would require a forensic analyst to figure out.
- owls and other birds we'd scare from their branches that would angrily swoop down upon us causing everyone to duck and raising shivers in the bravest of us.
- and the *piece de resistance*, a man-made cabin. It was as dark inside as it was outside. I was one of the few who went in. Tacked on a wall was a bible streaked with rivulets of blood There were satanic verses on the walls. Bodies of sacrificed animals, teeming with flies and maggots, were at the foot of an altar.

Remember, we were in the middle of nowhere. Only flashlights, which often cast a dim light, or backlit things, gave us a sight of the scenery. We had found the true house of horrors. *The Texas Chain Saw Massacre* comes to mind. What we didn't find was a child. The murders continued.

The irony of Williams' conviction is that prosecutors never tried Williams for the other 28 murders. No closure ever came for the parents of those children.

Catholic-Jewish Relations

We had to have each other's backs . . .

Let's lighten it up a bit and tell one more story, a different kind of story: "The Arch and the Jew." It's about how a Roman Catholic Archbishop, born and raised in the Bronx, came to Atlanta and met a Jewish kid from Brooklyn, who arrived a bit before him. Both discovered they were fish out of water. They took to each other, and exciting things happened. The Jew became the first non-Catholic to deliver a sermon at a Catholic Church. Big deal? Well, yes it was because it was against Church policy at the time. The archbishop didn't say yes, but then again, he didn't say no. He suggested that if such a thing were to occur, it might be better in a hall of religious education used for mass. He looked away, as it were. Sometimes, history is made when something isn't done as opposed to it being done. His looking away allowed the making of history.

In those days, when the "Arch" said jump, the bishops said "of course!" Maybe an explanation of hierarchy is needed here. The first rung is the priest. Next up is the Monsignor, a title given to a priest who has greater responsibilities than caring for his parish or oversees a particularly large and/or important church. Then we have a bishop to whom the priests of an area report and the archbishop to whom the bishops report. The cardinal, the red-cloaked fellow wearing a red beanie, is less a regional supervisor than a policy administrator for the Vatican. The Pope appoints cardinals. The cardinals, in conclave, pick the pope when the previous one dies or, more recently, retires. Got it?

"My" archbishop, Thomas Donnellan, had a province that covered the Carolinas, Georgia, and Tennessee. If memory serves, there were six bishops in the province. With a personal letter from Donnellan to each bishop, I had entry to every diocese for which he was responsible. The culmination of our work together was in the bi-centennial year. Each diocese was to do something to mark America's two hundredth year. Donnellan, socially progressive and theologically conservative, liked to think outside the box. He invited me to join all his bishops in a place I can only describe the way Loretta Lynn describes "Butcher Holler" in her award-winning cultural classic, *Coal Miner's Daughter*. Here are some references points:

- Born a coal miner's daughter
- Poor
- (Daddy) shoveled coal to make a poor man's dollar
- All day long in the field
- Read the Bible by the coal oil light
- Eight kids on a miner's pay
- Scrubbed clothes on a washboard every day
- Fingers bleed
- To complain, there was no need
- In the summertime, we didn't have shoes to wear
  But in the wintertime, we'd all get a brand-new pair
  Money made from selling a hog

None of my bishops had that kind of upbringing. I would guess few listened to that kind of music.

There, in a clearing in the woods, sat a long wooden table. Around it sat the robed bishops with the Arch in the middle. In this very evangelical and pentecostal spot on the map, the publicity machines of the Catholic Church spread the word. The bishops would be reaching out to people who had probably never seen a Catholic and who mostly thought of them, shall we say, poorly. They were "Papists!"

To what purpose was this gathering, you wonder? First of all, to open lines of communication. Secondly, to emphasize the brotherhood of faith. Thirdly, to see what folks needed that the Roman Catholic Church could provide. There was a big spread of food, the only seemingly Jewish touch to this Christian gathering . . . Everything was ready, but the holler stayed the way it was when we set up. Empty.

At first, no one showed up. The bishops grumbled, but Donnellan was confident. Then like spies in comic books, faces showed up from behind trees, then some folks stepped into the clearing and stared. Finally, a few sat down, and others followed.

I wish I could tell you that there was a breakthrough. There wasn't. But except for my attendance at a Billy Graham Crusade, it was one of my career's most interesting interfaith moments. Worry not, we'll get to Graham when we get to Miami.

Atlanta wasn't all there was to the job. Places like Memphis, Nashville, and Mobile, Alabama, provided happenings that created a sense in me of what Linus called "humbility." Here are a few examples.

●●●

AJC sent me to Atlanta to do two things. One, as I mentioned, was to fire the long-time secretary who a long time ago had become not so good at "secretarying." After about two weeks of working with her, that became easy.

The other was to put some life into our non-office chapters. I had a multi-state territory: North Carolina, South Carolina, Mississippi, Alabama, and Tennessee. Each was as different from the other as was the spelling of their names. Here's a sampling.

Alabama

BIRMINGHAM

The memory of Bull Connor's actions was front and center in everyone's minds.

In a state with a Jewish population of two-tenths of one percent, there's not much that can be done. Jews were dotted all over the place due to the peculiarity of Jewish migration and commercial patterns. There just were not a lot of them. Yet, they had an impact— for example, the Pizitz retail empire.

Pizitz was a major regional department store chain in Alabama with its flagship store in downtown Birmingham. At its peak, it operated 12 other stores, mainly in Birmingham, with several locations in Huntsville and other Alabama cities.

Louis De Pitz (sorry I don't know when or why the spelling changed) founded the company in 1899 on the site of its flagship building in downtown Birmingham. Sold to McRae's in December 1986, all former Pizitz stores became McRae's. In its day, the name Pizitz was one to be reckoned with in the world of retailing from New York's garment district to the heart of the south.

In the 1970s, Birmingham was a very southern community in all the worst ways. It was Bull Conner, it was fire hoses, it was segregation, it was George Wallace. Yet, in its homes and offices, it was gentility. It frowned upon cursing. Men wore suits and ties, women dresses. It was *Driving Miss Daisy*. The Jewish community was no different, except it was a southern community inside a southern community.

There was a definite five o'clock shadow. Even if you were Mr. Pizitz, you were first known as a Jew, sometimes in conversation, ". . . Mr. Pizitz, the Jew," or to some, ". . . the Jew, Pizitz." There is a strong difference between the two constructions.

Retailing in the south followed an interesting and relatively common story. Jewish immigrant peddlers, often fresh off the boat, decided to head for greener pastures, literally and figuratively. They ended up in places like Birmingham, Atlanta, Greensboro, Miami, and Mobile, to mention a few. Like Richard Rich of Atlanta, they started with pushcarts. Adept at learning which kinds of people needed what kind of fare, they prospered. Soon, instead of chasing their customers, they picked a spot, and their customers sought them out. Eventually, Mr. Rich bought a plot of land, built a building, opened the store, and populated the southland over two or three decades with Jewish clothing retailers and jewelers. Some were Rich family members; some were part of Rich enterprises.

Before returning to Birmingham, let me regale you with my favorite story. It is a Jewish take on *The Beverly Hillbillies*. The Friedman family of Mobile were the town jewelers. Poppa bought a piece of land far out of town just because he thought being a landowner was a good idea, an investment. Little did he know how right he was.

Times were not easy; the property taxes were burdensome, so Poppa was going to sell. A friend told him not to. Do a survey, his lawyer counseled. Long story short—liquid gold. Multi-millionaires, the Friedman's became investors in multiple projects around the country, owning for a time the luxurious Hay-Adams Hotel, two blocks from the White House.

Back in Birmingham, what happened at my first luncheon meeting was *deja vue* all over again. Even so, when it happened, it still was a bit of a shock. My host was a real estate magnate whose family had old and deep roots in town and with AJC. I brought one of our best from what we called "National." David Geller, a scholar on antisemitism and a gentleman, was my choice. Also, an Orthodox

Jew. I thought letting him know would be the right thing to do, and all the explanation about the lunch menu I would need. Wrong.

The Executive Dining Room at Mr. Engle's building was posh, whistle clean, replete with black staff and plantation manners. Of course, white gloves. We sat down and chatted about AJC and our wants and needs from Birmingham. Mr. Geller would speak after lunch; one served with high banquet precision. The first course was hot soup, even though it was mid-summer and sauna-like outside. The staff put before Mr. Geller a steaming, fragrant red broth. He looked at it suspiciously. There was "stuff" floating around in the white china soup bowls. Geller asked, "What is this, if you please?" The answer? "Why, it's She-crab soup, suh." Then, again with the shrimp, this time gigantic ones in cocktail glasses. Double whammy. My eyes began to roll back in my head. I muttered to myself, "Turn off the oven, I'm done."

GADSDEN

Gadsden is a small city with big minded folks.

The Engle family gave and raised money for us. They were known far and wide. Something else I wanted was to broaden my reach into Alabama. I wanted contacts. Engle was the man I needed for that. What I got was fascinating. For example, he directed me to a family in Gadsden, Alabama. Then Alabama's fourth largest city, Gadsden was a large village by east coast standards. There, a rabbi and an Episcopal priest joined forces after an outbreak of antisemitism. They developed multiple programs cooperating with AJC to bring together their congregations, their families, and the community. It worked. Too well? No opinion, just the facts. The Rabbi's daughter and the priest's son fell in love and got married. 'probably more success than either clergyman anticipated—or probably hoped for.

ANNISTON

**If you want to know what the average guy thinks,
then go to where he goes, and listen.**

Another meeting was to be with H. Brandt (Brandy) Ayers, the owner/publisher of the Anniston *Alabama Star*. The Ayers family and its paper went back a hundred years, fighting segregation and editorializing against its evils. Ayers was among the most interesting and intelligent people I'd ever met. I learned two things from him. One was about writing. Ayers wrote the most amazing first sentences

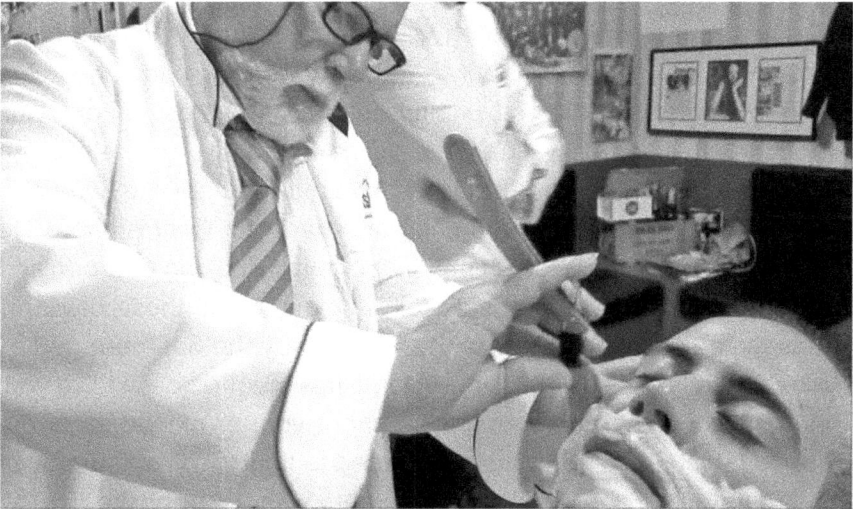

When he wanted to take the pulse of the town, he went and sat in the barbershop.

I'd ever read. You began his column, and that first sentence whisked you through the entire editorial. He'd say, "People are impatient." Get'em quick, or they're gone." The second was to listen. Ayers' favorite place for getting the community pulse was the barbershop. He'd sometimes drop in without needing a haircut to sit and listen. Brandy Ayers knew what was cookin' in Anniston, what folks thought about it, and what was happening around it.

Anniston was a small town. He felt it needed something. With his wife, he decided what it needed was a Shakespeare festival. Anyone who was a bettin' man would have bet against its success. Anniston is probably the smallest town with a well-reviewed Shakespeare festival. Ayers is long gone; the last I heard, the festival is not.

Brandy Ayers provided one of the most wonderful intellectual hours of my life. At an AJC meeting, an interview program featured him with Morris Abram, a Jewish son of the south and former Nuremberg prosecutor. To hear these men ruminate over the troubles of people and the world they lived in was a heady experience, especially for a 29-year-old. It was like being transported to the room in heaven where the smart folks hung out.

Like so many important men with power, Brandy Ayers had clay feet. I was stunned and deeply saddened when I read a headline about an accusation of sexual misconduct. The last time I was in touch with him, he wasn't himself and seemed to be telling me something was amiss that I couldn't quite put together. He had been chasing a skirt, caught it, fondled it, was sued, and lost his paper. He seemed ok. He spent a lot of time on the porch drinking bourbon and reflecting on life. Near as I could tell, as many did in those days, his wife saw the scandal as part of the life lived by the Southern gentry. Brooklyn, I think, is easier to understand. If someone doesn't like you, they tell you off, punch you, maybe shoot you, or maybe all of the above. Not much deep thought is needed to figure it all out. Brooklyn is a drama with thin plots. The Deep South was the opposite.

Tennessee

CHATTANOOGA

Rattlesnakes in church . . . I didn't get that kind of worship.

Chattanooga has raw hills surrounding it, carpet mills, the choo-choo, an odd bunch of snake-handling Christians, and a gigantic cross erected overlooking the highway below. That cross said, "Around here

. . . give me my dog any day and twice on Sundays
(Photo by Russell Lee 1946)

there ain't no separation of church and state." It turned out that the issue was bigger than me, a lot. It's probably still there. And the snake handling? Rattlesnakes were plentiful in the Tennessee mountains. I didn't get that kind of worship and still don't. I mean, I have nothing against snakes, except the pythons in the Everglades, but to reach into a cage, pick up a few, and hold them high in worship offerings to God? Never saw that in any synagogue, nor church for that matter. And it was all part of God's plan if, as did happen, a snake was not in the mood for worship and latched onto the worshipper's face or arm, requiring an immediate trip to the hospital for anti-venom injections. Some churches packed their own serum. Some did neither. Whether or not the person died was to be God's judgment on them. I don't need to get that kind of reprimand from God, thank you very much. There were many more snakes in Chattanooga than Jews. It didn't seem like fertile land to plant seeds of religious compatibility.

NASHVILLE

The Klan was born forty miles away . . . and was active again.

I haven't been back in years, but Nashville then was a small mountain town that was country music heaven. It had many side streets, small bars, and clubs where young hopefuls performed. Occasionally, an "already made" personality would drop in to try out some new songs. There were, of course, established clubs like Tootsie's Orchid Lounge, the oldest honky-tonk in town. Many stars have their own clubs: AJ's (Alan Jackson), Chief's (Eric Church), and the Ryman Auditorium, the mecca of the industry and the original home to the Grand Ole Opry. You sat in an auditorium with excellent acoustics for a reasonable price and saw a vaudeville version of the industry. For the price of admission, you got stars who sang, bands that played, and comedians whose humor dug down into the roots of

Grand Ole Opry: Where Country Music Fans Want to Go When They Die.

country life. Minnie Pearl, retail price tag hanging from her hat, and her famous opening line, "Howwwww-deee!" was one. Jerry Clower was so "Mississippi farm," you were surprised he didn't do his act standing next to a hog.

●●●

My mission in Nashville? To ask the undisputed Jewish community leader, Mr. Bernard (pronounced (Ber-nid) Werthan, whom my predecessor had somehow mishandled, to give us another shot with me in charge. "Crusty" would be an understatement to describe his usual demeanor. I was advised not to talk until he opened the conservation. I was additionally advised that my approach should be honest, direct, short, and obsequious.

After a short wait, I arrived at Werthan Industries and entered Mr. Werthan's office. I remember a big man behind a big desk, smoking a big cigar, and having a commanding, big head of hair. "Lion" is the image that came to mind, followed by the thought of getting eaten if I failed. Motioned to a chair, I sat. Already seated and not getting up, he perused me. My heart was pounding like a jackhammer. Mr. Werthan finally said something. One word with a question mark. "So?"

followed by a large, empty, silent space containing one sound—the tick-tock of the office's clock. Eerie. I followed the script. I made my pitch . . . or plea. At its end, he said, "Ok, we'll give it another try." Had I not had other meetings, I would have gone, again, directly to a bar to calm nerves as taut as fiddle strings.

Nashville is an interesting place. Twice in the airport, I saw recording stars waiting for their luggage. In those days, "star sightings" were pretty frequent. I met the head of CBS records, a name I knew because I was a country and western music fan. One of my board members was "the accountant to the stars." One of the stars was Johnny Cash, but my work in Nashville mainly involved combating the Klan. It would have been enough if that work was all I ever did in my career. See if you don't agree.

As a reaction to the country's social upheaval, Klans around the country began coming to life. In a small Alabama town, a Klan rally drew thousands of people. The issue was the rape of a white woman by a black man. It turned out that the man had a mentally disabled twin, and it was he who had committed the crime. For me, the issue was the Klan's revival and what to do about it. Born 40 miles from Nashville by Confederate General Nathan Bedford Forrest, the Klan was an everyday part of life in that area. He had established a social network for Confederate soldiers trying to recover themselves, their families, and their businesses from the loss of the Civil War. Then came Reconstruction and radicalization. The Klan became a hotbed of hostility and resentment. I had a brainstorm.

In Nashville was a storied, liberal newspaper run by a storied, liberal journalist. It was the *Nashville Tennessean*. His name was John Seigenthaler. He was Tennessean through and through, having started on the lowest rung of the highest ladder, climbing to its very top. He not only held the responsibility for the paper's history but was Chairman of the Robert F. Kennedy Memorial Book Prize. He was a deputy working with RFK when his assassination occurred.

I later learned that Seigenthaler was a prize I didn't know I had in my territory. He had two sides. In the newsroom, he was a perfectionist who could be very prickly. One of his reporters who showed great promise was not reaching it as fast as his boss thought he could and should. A Pulitzer Prize winner for his book, *The Best and the Brightest*, David Halberstam, became so infuriated at the heckling from Seigenthaler that he rose from his desk, grabbed his typewriter, and threw it at him! The other side was the man who took my wife and me to one of the finest dinners we'd ever eaten. He wore his signature Corum gold watch and drank his only drink, Champagne. He was as gracious a host as I've ever encountered. Conversation came to him as easily as breathing. He had the genius for scoping out the interests of those he was with and speaking to those subjects. And he was a wonderfully entertaining storyteller.

It was this man I decided to call for an appointment, and with no effort at all, I made a total fool out of myself. How? I informed this marvelous intellect, this man of the world, this legend in journalism that the KKK had been founded virtually at his doorstep, a bit south of Nashville in Pulaski, Tennessee, that there had recently been this rape of a white woman in Decatur, Alabama, creating an uber Klan rally, and wouldn't it be a great opportunity for the paper to cover the resurgence? He sat there looking at me, seemingly in rapt deep interest. All of this I said to one of the most famous journalists in America. In the end, he thanked me for bringing him the story, it seemed to have merit, and he'd get back to me in a few weeks. It wasn't until I learned what he'd come up with that made me realize how much of a fool I had made of myself and how generous he was with his patience.

I got a call to come back, and here's what he laid out. When shown into Seigenthaler's office this time, three people were waiting for me, along with the boss. One was the newspaper's librarian. One was the newspaper's head of research, and the third was the newspaper's crack investigative reporter. His name was Jerry Thompson. We would come to know each other well. We forged a relationship that would last until his death.

Here's the plan. This team of three would fly to Atlanta and use my office as a base. Mind you, would use, not ask to use. There, they would put together an exposé of the Klan's rise with my input and access to my files. Were this successful, the paper would plan to go after the Klan directly. I was astonished and spellbound. As they say, this would be something special to tell the grandkids.

They were there for about three weeks. The phones burned with their constant calls. Mostly, they were out more than they were in. Hurried flights to different parts of the south. Drives to meets in Georgia. I'd liken it to a squad running a mission. I knew little about what they accomplished when they packed up and departed. This was going to be a bombshell, and they didn't want any leaks. In a few more weeks, the paper began to promote a coming exposé of Klan activity. What they first produced was a magazine insert. It began with the history of the Klan, covered its ups and downs, and finally

The Klan in Chicago—and you were sure it was Mississippi.

delved deeply into the cause and effects of the Alabama rally. It was a gem. Several weeks later, came another call.

This time waiting in the office with Seigenthaler were two people, one was the corporation counsel, the second was Thompson. Astonished by the first go-round, I was struck dumb by what was to come. Thompson, who looked the part of a Klansman, was built like a bull, had a florid complexion, and a bald pate. He would infiltrate the Klan. His job was to do his investigative thing and cause as much disruption as possible. Seigenthaler said only the three of us would know what Thompson was doing and where he was doing it. Not even was his wife included in the loop. She only knew he would be on a long-term assignment. We would never mention his name on the phone. That led to some very odd-sounding coded conversations.

Then came the lawyer. Thompson would establish a false identity like an undercover cop's. He would check in as little as possible, had an emergency code if he needed extraction or other kinds of help. Most importantly, the lawyer said to Jerry, "Although you are doing a good thing for a good purpose, when you are with the Klan you are, for all intents and purposes, a Klansman." If they were to test Thompson by having him do something illegal or if he were out on a Klan operation like setting a bomb at a church, if guns were involved—in sum, if he got caught doing something illegal, he could be arrested and prosecuted for the crime. There would be no wink and a nod, no get-out-of-jail-free card. The paper could do nothing for him except handle his defense. Thompson would not only have to come up with a convincing cover, but he would also have to be nimble afoot, and mind, so as not to end up on the wrong side of the law. Here's what he came up with.

●●●

A middle Tennessee country boy, Thompson was good with his hands. He settled himself in a small town and took a job as an assistant to a cabinet maker. He'd never made a cabinet in his life. With thick arms and a broad back there was much he could do in terms of getting supplies and delivering cabinets. He was pretty good at it and with stops at neighborhood bars after work, he began to be known in the area. The paper deposited his paycheck in Nashville, so he wasn't under financial strain. A single man, Army vet, running from family troubles, or so the story went, Thompson spent his nights at the bars, which was second nature to him anyway. As I learned after the story broke and we traveled the circuit a bit, he could drink an elephant under the table. But this time, there was a purpose to the bars and the boozing. Thompson's persona was a man angry at society, angry at the country, and anxious to do his part to right things in the world. The Klan soon found him.

It was a slow process just like it would be in a movie. Meet this person, then that one. If you passed muster with them, there were others. There were meetings to attend, rallies to go to. Constantly having to know what he was going to have to do without raising suspicions was nerve-racking. The words of the lawyer rang in his ears. There was no safety net between him and jail. A final warning was that he would be infiltrating David Duke's Klan. Duke was changing his persona. Urbane, well-dressed, and well-spoken, he would know to vet Jerry thoroughly. The manufactured bio had to be airtight and memorized so that Jerry himself could believe it. Finally, came the induction.

The rest of the story is so gutsy, so fraught with danger, that four decades later, I still can't believe he pulled it off, no less thought of it. Part of it is explained in Seigenthaler's preface to the resultant book, *My Life in the Klan*. Thompson looked the part. He was a soft-voiced man of the soil, from economic circumstances similar to those he would be befriending. And, said Seigenthaler, he looked like a redneck. The meld into the community should be fairly easy.

Thompson allies himself with David Duke's wing of the Klan. Duke had already begun to build a more moderate image for himself, a more cerebral type of Klan, and an organization that would put him in front of audiences around the country, the world, and eventually into politics. He turned in his sheet for a suit and tie. His racist rhetoric became far more nuanced. He was becoming a star. Word was that Duke was headed off to greener pastures in a new Duchy.

Understand, there were plenty of true believers left. Duke's main rival was Bill Wilkinson, who was from the axe-handle end of the Klan movement. He criticized Duke mercilessly. Thompson moved in that direction. He brokered a meeting between Duke and Wilkinson in a backwoods cabin. Slyly, he had set up audio equipment furtively squirreled away in its nooks and crannies.

At a table in the center, David Duke had agreed to sell his Klan. Hopefully, you see the irony of an anti-black segregationist selling his lily-white organization like so much chattel. Within hours, the informal wires of communication were crackling. Duke was a turncoat. Jerry had taken on the two biggest Klan organizations in the south, turned them on their heads, and rendered them chaotic. Not bad for an assistant cabinetmaker.

Life after the Klan was at times as hairy as life in it. Death threats were constant. Even I, mentioned around two dozen times in his book, received a death threat from another rising Klan kingpin, Don Black. Black, best known for leading the raid on Grenada, had charted his own course after the Duke/Wilkinson split. He was a tall, lean, mean man who didn't live too far from me in Florida.

Once Jerry's book came out, we hit the speaker's circuit. Security experts had warned us never to get

My Life in the Klan author, *Jerry Thompson, in dark glasses, a reporter for Nashville newspaper,* The Tennessean, *infiltrated the Ku Klux Klan.*

into our cars without looking underneath them. We were told not to turn on the ignition if anything looked tampered with. Giving a speech was Jerry's way of warming up for drinking time; that's how I learned about his capacity for liquor. There were nights he drank me into semi-paralysis. Parts of my body seemed to unplug themselves from my nervous system. They were AWOL. The mornings were God-awful. After a good bender, Jerry would sleep like a log. One morning, I learned something about body chemistry. A person can drink so much that hours later, the booze can be smelled coming from his pores. Nature's "hair of the dog?"

This escapade was also hard on Jerry's new wife and kids. It was bad enough when he was away, managing every few months to slip home for a night, but at the end of the assignment, a flood-lit fence was erected about the house, turning it into a compound with regular police patrols.

I say to you, try to live a normal life fenced in and lit up like that.

Here's a P.S. to the story. There was this deep south "surprise" Jerry shared with me. A key supporter of David Duke and his Klan was a wealthy, rural medical doctor. He had his own plane and ferried Duke thither and yon. Not my kind of medical man. But such surprises have lasted 'til this very day, so often they aren't surprises anymore.

There is a PPS to the story. You'll find it when we get to Miami, but I digress. In the category of, "Why Do Bad Things Happen to Good People?" Jerry developed cancer. Yet he soldiered on—for eleven years. He worked until he no longer could, then he sat on the porch, looking at nature, the Klan fence long gone.

I don't remember how many operations he had or how many chemo and radiation treatments he suffered through. I stopped counting at eleven surgeries. Surgeons removed so many things from his insides, I thought if he swallowed a marble, it would make the sounds of a xylophone as it bounced around his ribs. His insurance ran out. The paper held a fund-raiser for him. My wife and I visited him in a Nashville hospital. He was the same old Jerry, although the meat on his frame was gone. He was gaunt, knew it was the end, but faced it head-on. I can't count the number of things I learned from this simple, complex, intuitive man nor measure what I owe him. It saddens me that Jerry was dealing with an embryo of hate that, despite his 18-month effort, has grown today into something unimaginable. And I still don't have the answer to the question. Why do bad things happen to good people?

MEMPHIS

As I left his office, the president of FEDEX said to me, "Scrape together as much money as you can spare and invest it in my company."
I thought he was kidding.

Then we have Memphis, Queen of the Mississippi, and her jazz. AJC had a chapter there, and its head was a retired Jewish Marine, the first of those I'd ever met. Memphis was the kind of town that was nice to you if you minded your own business. It is also the home of FedEx, where I had gone to seek its founder, Fred Smith, another Marine but not Jewish, to help raise funds for us by receiving a

Kiaweh Island: Motel 6 it ain't.

community service award at a gala dinner. He declined. But he had some advice for me. "Scrape together whatever money you can get your hands on and buy stock in my company." I thought he was playing with me. I had hit him up for money. He was turning the tables. I never considered it. Had I, I could have been a millionaire. Oh well, there's always Powerball.

Jewish researchers had discovered a pattern in the viability of smaller Jewish communities. When out-migration began to occur, eventually the community would cease to be a community and instead would be a collection of Jews. Synagogues would shrink, combine, and close as would Jewish schools and community centers. This became a subject of conversation at the Memphis Federation. AJC was involved because it was the only major agency that had a department devoted to Jewish communal affairs. Were there signals we could divine that would tell us the future of Memphis' Jewish community?

I took this discussion back to the department's director. We decided research was the answer but who would do it? Brainstorm. Georgia State University. It was an urban university, had a full research complement, and was interested in demographics and other urban patterns. After a meeting or two with some of the University's key researchers, they became enthusiastic about the idea. But what was the idea?

With input from the Memphis and Nashville professional leadership, the Georgia State folks with AJC put together a questionnaire. The Federations agreed to mail the survey to all their members, as did AJC in Atlanta. I believe we included Macon and Savannah. The returns would be analyzed by creating punch cards and running them through the computers. When I look at the punch cards and what was printed out, I realized how primitive this research was. Yet, while it produced nothing really earth-shaking, it did produce interesting and important patterns.

It matched previous larger studies but it gave the communities a snapshot of Jewish participation—an idea of how many people identified as Jews, how many were "just Jews" and how many practicing Jews, what were the things Jewish that most people identified with. The answers to these questions and others enabled the planners to create programs that would better speak to the "wants" of the community. For its time, it was an important work. Without overemphasizing my role, I do want to point out that the Atlanta, Memphis, and Nashville Jewish communities are still there and still strong.

●●●

Memphis is as different from Nashville as Chicago is from New York. Memphis' roots are riverboat roots. Memphis didn't have country and western from which its persona was cobbled; it was the town of the Blues. As there was a "Bernid Werthin" in Nashville, there was a "Mr. Abe" in Memphis. The rest of Mr. Abe was "Plough." He was the Plough of the Plough-Shearing Corporation. Little happened in the Jewish community that Mr. Abe didn't approve. Little happened in the city that might impact the Jewish community without the town fathers reaching out to this King of the Jews. Elvis was one kind of King, Mr. Abe another.

Memphis was a real southern town. It didn't have the spunkiness and spring-in-the-step of Nashville's mountain tempo. Things in Memphis were done slowly, deliberately, often by a handshake or by giving one's word. Memphis was one bridge away from the Mississippi River to the state of the same name. There wasn't a dime's worth of difference besides the alphabet between the two. The Catholic Church recognized this by including that part of Mississippi in the Diocese of Memphis.

I wish I could remember her name. She was the bishop's everything; you didn't get to meet him before you met her. Most probably, she decided if someone needed to see him or if she could handle whatever it was. If you knew the Memphis diocese, you knew she was the power behind the throne. "Behind every good man is a better woman." She was nothing if not gracious, welcoming, and

WILLIAM A. GRALNICK

protective. As I think back, I want to call her Sister Grace, dressed in black with a fresh, white rose pinned every day anew to her jacket. I came to like her, and she me. We talked a lot about life as well as business. Every project idea I had, she honed to his liking and his benefit. When the bishop made one of the most courageous stands any modern American bishop made, I backed him in and out of the press. That, dear reader, is foreshadowing.

We, she and I, decided that the bishop should hold a meet and greet for the Jewish leadership at his home. It was a Southern mansion. Some bishops lived like priests, others a bit better. The Archbishop of Miami lived in a typical Miami Gardens "four/three" with an add-on conference room. He used the Archdiocese offices for almost all his work. If you got invited home, you would have passed his test of trust. I got invited home. More foreshadowing.

This Bishop's home was very "Southern mansion." His welcome was country club lavish. All that I remember of it was "the welcome." Here's why. Guests entered the home into a foyer that was eye-stopping. From the ceiling hung a huge and stunning chandelier. At the front door with "Sister Grace" stood the bishop. Behind him was a six-foot, maybe taller, falling water ice fountain. Sitting on the ice was more shrimp than I had ever seen, except maybe at a fish market. For the uninitiated, shrimp is not kosher. One should not serve it at formal functions for Jews. I was speechless. On the other hand, most of the attendees chowed down without a thought.

Fitting for Memphis, not much of any great note took place in my work except that Mr. Abe sold Plough-Shearing and was now no longer rich; he was a gazillionaire. Then came the bishop's "whoops!"

Carrol T. Dozier, whose career ended in disgrace, was the first bishop of Memphis. He was a liberal both socially and theologically. He came out against the Vietnam War and spoke on behalf of busing as a tool for school desegregation. Most noted for holding a Mass of Reconciliation, Dozier held two, much to the dissatisfaction of Pope Paul VI, who appointed him.

Like most deep south bishops, Dozier was up against a tide of Evangelical Protestantism. The power of the Southern Baptist Convention was incontrovertible. Southern Methodists were not far behind. There were small Pentecostal churches everywhere. Protestantism fit far more easily the lives of rural, poor people than Roman Catholicism. All one needed was a Bible and a chair, and you could do without the chair. At best, the state was about 4% Catholic. How, he pondered, could he bring the once faithful back to church, people lost mostly through divorce? He decided evangelism would not do it. He had to get back the folks who had once experienced the church in their life.

There were many people who were divorced Catholics. They would be his primary target. The Mass of Reconciliation succinctly is a mass of forgiveness. For the attendees, it forgave things that were sins, violations of the church's dogma. It was a mass for a mass of sinners. He got called to the Vatican. There are several reasons a priest goes to the Vatican. One is an invitation. Another is to be called. Dozier was called and spent several weeks being "re-tooled" in dogma and returned a chastened man. But it would get worse.

He retired a few years later due to "ill health." I had serious doubts about that. He seemed ok to me, just aging. I wanted to reach out and say a kind word. It was impossible. No one except the inner circle knew where he was. No one was allowed to visit. Without an address, one couldn't send mail. I know; I tried. I spoke to bishops I knew. I got nowhere. Every piece I had on the board was blocked by one the church had placed.

And it would get "worser" yet. Dozier had headed three parishes in Richmond, Va., before becoming Bishop. The announcement came that he was one of several priests in the Richmond Diocese "credibly" accused of pedophilia. He "disappeared" after his retirement, along with any trace of him. The powers that be in the church erased his name from anything it appeared on. Even a beautiful mural that spoke to the good he did, flowed down street drains under the force of power sprayers.

WILLIAM A. GRALNICK

Pedophilia is unforgivable. It is a terrible sin. Yet, isn't every person entitled to be treated as a human, given comfort, allowed to find some grace in the Lord's presence? I feel yes is the answer. It was easier for the church to paper over the real problem in the priesthood, the intake process of priests, and the need for psychological testing done repeatedly throughout the stages of a priest's career. Instead, it focused just on the crime and the man who committed it. There was to be no reconciliation for Carrol T. Dozier. On July 27, 1982, his resignation letter to Pope Paul lowered the final curtain.

North Carolina

GREENSBORO

. . . service was by white-gloved black people whose vocabulary
seemed restricted to yes and no with sir or ma'am tacked on.

On the highway into Greensboro, I learned that not all the trailers dotting the highways and byways were for construction. Some were, well, whorehouses. One learns such things at truck stops.

I met a Jewish family that sounded like no other Jewish family I'd ever heard pronounce the English language. At a family dinner in my honor, service was by white-gloved, black people whose vocabulary seemed restricted to "yes or no" with "ma'am" or "suh" tacked on. From my perspective, the host's grandparents were on the wrong side of the civil war.

I worked hard to involve myself in the work of the three institutions on a corner of downtown, Presbyterian, Catholic, and Jewish. The leaders of their flocks were all good men, enjoyable to be with, and deeply committed to the kind of social issues that were the hallmark of my organization. One day the reality that my work had paid off came via an invitation from the presbyterian minister for me to speak at Sunday services.

In those days, the Presbyterian Church was two separate and unequal branches. The Southern Presbyterians called the shots; they were the conservatives, religiously and politically, and a much larger institution than their northern brethren. To have anyone who wasn't Southern Presbyterian give the Sunday sermon called for in the minds of some the use of public stocks for the minister, center city whipping, maybe even burning at the stake for the speaker. I exaggerate—but not so much.

I prepared long and hard for my historic day. Sunday morning, I met the minister. He would lead me to the podium and introduce me. Nothing seemed odd until we got into an elevator. We rode up two floors and stepped out onto the podium. The sermonizer walked the plank, a narrow pathway that opened into a small circle. On that perch stood the speaker, an entire floor above the parishioners. I was generously introduced, put aside my fear of heights, and walked the plank. Suddenly reality hit me. The church was very 19th century, stunning in its classic, forbidding style. And it was big. The house was packed, and I was perched above them, shaking like a leaf. The post-Reformation history of this church smacked me in the face. I was out of place.

Mind you, I was an experienced and practiced speaker. I had a carefully crafted message that wove Hebrew and Christian Bible elements into a theme of community and grace through "love thy neighbor." The only problem was that I was so unsettled by the setting that I froze. That had never happened before. Call it a "Mitch McConnel." It was a long enough freeze that some of the peoples' expectations were becoming questions about this kid above them, and worse yet, a tad (very southern expression) irritated. I knew I had to break the mood and would if I could only get something to come out of my mouth. Seemingly on its own, bursting through my lips, came this: "Along with my mother, many of you are thinking, *What's a nice Jewish boy doing in a place like this*?" Ba da boom. It worked. I got a big laugh and was off to the races. I got great reviews—except from the group of people who signed a petition calling for the pastor's termination.

Something extraordinary came from it all. The two churches and the synagogue saw an opportunity begging for recognition. I brought the clergy together to establish a program of rotating sermons and the development of a special Thanksgiving service. Each year, a different house of worship would host it. AJC had made its mark.

Another tidbit. When I was responsible for North Carolina, you didn't have to be a lawyer to become the state's Attorney General. You only needed the most votes. I did see someone elected in a primary to run for that position who was not a lawyer. It turned out as badly as you might imagine.

There was something else afoot across the land. Cults. Kids lured into communes, indoctrinated to believe their leader was divine, God-like, and theirs was to do his bidding. The leader told kids who to marry and forced them to do it—often in their teens. Some of the leaders kept a harem of youngsters. Others made it mandatory that the initiate sleep with the leader as the final acceptance into the cult.

There were prayer sessions that included group sex, "free love." There were illegal activities to get the money to sustain the commune. There were legal but annoying fund-raising activities. Remember the Hare Krishnas in the airports and on the streets? Health care was non-existent, so was communicating with the outside world, including parents. And everyone had Jonestown on their minds.

My colleague, Rabbi A. James Rudin, studied, wrote, and lectured extensively on this phenomenon. He and his wife, Marsha, were two of a small handful of true experts on the subject. The Greensboro Jewish community saw Jewish kids disappearing into the night; they asked for help. We reached out to several churches to find out they had their kids brainwashed away from community, church, and family. We brought Rudin in for a talk held in a huge, packed church basement. Fear, worry, anxiety, and terror were palpable in the room. Like the loss of the silverware and everything it meant mentioned before in Atlanta, outreach programs to parents about the loss of their children were heart-rending. Getting to the kids required investigators, law enforcement, and lawyers. Sometimes deprogramming a child worked. Often it did not.

And that was the lasting takeaway. Oh yes, there were committees and task forces, programs, and projects but what hit me so hard was the gathering of a hundred or more parents all scared *in extremis* for their children. It was one of those things a person doesn't understand until becoming a parent.

This is the story of my awakening as a parent might feel if he/she felt their child had disappeared. When he was five, during the Atlanta child murder period, my son and I became separated in a shopping mall. He was there, by my side, until he wasn't. I learned what the expression "to have one's blood run cold" meant. He did what I had taught him. He found a policeman, and I found them fooling around together. Suddenly the adrenaline was gone; I felt like a water balloon with no water. FOR TEN MINUTES THE CLOCK STOPPED ON MY LIFE. Thank goodness, all was well and ended well.

In conclusion, I guess one could say belonging to a Klan was like belonging to an adult cult. At a face off outside Greensboro between the Klan and opponents who had come to disrupt a rally, I learned that it takes only one person with a gun to cause murder and mayhem. To see such happenings now is shockingly routine. Witnessing them both scared the bejeezus out of me and taught me never to underestimate the potential for danger by the size of a crowd.

South Carolina

GREENVILLE

Then came the purchase of Kiawah Island by the Saudis . . .
and a no-Jews-allowed restricted covenant.

Greenville, South Carolina, has Liberty University. So conservatively Christian it was that men and women were not allowed to hold hands in public. Kissing? Fuggedbodit. Interracial dating was unthinkable, and same-sex partnerships might be punished by hanging in front of the dormitories. Of course not, but the atmosphere created such thoughts. You can deduce that the left-of-center social policies of the American Jewish Committee were, at best, suspect.

Had anyone there found out that we had genuine live socialists on AJC'S staff in New York, the odds on my safety whilst in South Carolina would not have been good.

Liberty for WHO? WHOM?

Mississippi

JACKSON

It would take more than a firestorm to get me to go back.

The Mighty Miss

●●●

I wrote it off. There are just so many bottles and so much lightning. One guy can do just so much. I took one trip to Jackson, not arriving in a fever, to visit the rabbi. Red neck, Neo-Nazi vandals struck his synagogue (the Oath Takers and Proud Boys' forerunners). To show the flag, I left him with the hollow message, "If you need me, just call, and I'll be there." I was happy to let the Southern Poverty Law Center have the glory. Besides, having their lives threatened was "another day in the life of" for them.

Book Three

The AJC Years

Best speech in worst Spanish—Guatemala

Miami

**To this day you can be born, live a full life, and be
buried without ever having to learn English.**

People ask me how I ended up there. I tell them, "The guy who signs my checks sent me there." It was a similar story to my mission in Atlanta. Multiple complaints were coming in about the Miami office. I was sent to evaluate. I wrote a report, and got a phone call that said, "no one better than you to fix it." I had to go down there to meet the leadership. I stayed on the top floor of a classic downtown hotel. My room with a balcony overlooked Biscayne Bay. That night I learned why Miami is called the Magic City. The downtown was quite compact. Several buildings had colorful light displays, and the inter-county rail system's above-ground tracks that knifed through downtown had neon lights that ran the length of the track structure. It was a wow. Then I heard thunder.

Miami is in the sub-tropics. Living there often makes you wonder why climatologists added the "sub." It is hot and humid. Sometimes, it seems that things grow while you watch them. Thunderstorms are frequent, dramatic, and dangerous events. The thunder can shake the biggest of buildings. And the lightning! South Florida has more lightning strikes than the rest of the country combined. It also has the highest number of deaths from lightning strikes.

I've always loved watching storms, so the thunder was calling me to step out on the balcony. I watched these gigantic clouds forming over the Bay. The lightning within would light them up like explosions. As the clouds developed, arrows of lightning would knife from them and fork toward the water. Sometimes, several clouds would put on a show at the same time. Suddenly, I understood peoples' fears of the mythological god, Thor. What I was watching looked like Thor was launching bolts of electricity at the terrified non-believers below. And then came the rain. It came down so hard and fast that it appeared Thor had added a new weapon to his arsenal—waterfalls. In Texas, they called them "frog stranglers." I had a front-row seat to the drama of Mother Nature. I loved it.

Hurricane Andrew

The famous Brickell Ave. was block after block of glass skyscrapers and condos.

What was left of the Country Walk residential neighborhood after Hurricane Andrew.

●●●

Let's take a moment to reflect on what it's like when that drama encircles you. That's called a hurricane. We've had a bunch, but Hurricane Andrew (8/24/92) is the measure of those that came before and after. It was so bad that it changed the demographics, and the building codes, of South Florida. Let's start with the weather forecast.

Hurricane Andrew caused the weather forecasters fits. Every time it seemed to be aimed deadeye at a part of the peninsula, it changed its mind. If you look at a map of Florida's east coast, you'll see areas of the coast have names—The Treasure Coast, The Space Coast, The Gold Coast. Andrew headed for each one and, each time kept going south. The entire coast was on pins and needles. When the forecast said direct hit on Miami, homeowners boarded up hundreds of miles of houses and businesses along the coast with thousands of pounds of plywood following what folks had done up the coast. Those that had them closed the aluminum storm shutters. There were runs in stores on pretty much every item that was non-perishable and still on the shelves. In Home Depots, you'd be lucky to find a toothpick left; in supermarkets the shelves were bare. It would get worse. Understand, above and below the direct part of the hit were dozens of miles of fearsome storm. More unnerving was the fact that Andrew was wider east to west than the peninsula. Everybody was going to get something and that something wasn't going to be good.

In Boca, we knew that even if it didn't hit us, as reported, we'd get slammed anyway. The storm was frighteningly big. We lived in the kind of house that looked great because it was so unusual. Three

Hurricane strikes home.

of the interior hallways faced outside to the swimming pool. The water shimmered at you no matter where you were walking in the house. Unusual is not always good. In the summer, the heat from the reflection off the pool was so hot, it felt like you could get fried. All of those vantage points had 12-foot sliding glass doors. I had to board them all up.

The house came with the most primitive shutter system I'd ever seen. They were boards. Each window needed several sections of boards, and not one set was cut the same size as the others. This was a problem; I don't do jigsaw puzzles. I schlepped these boards in from the garage and laid them out on the patio. The heat and humidity were miserable. The wind was picking up, and it had begun to rain. I had to figure out which board went where and then, holding it up with pressure from one hand, use the drill to screw it into a pre-drilled hole in the house. Since it had been years between storms, the holes held years of dirt.

I had come to the point of desperation when our daughter came home from school. She walked out to the patio and asked how I was doing. I told her. She's very good at spatial relations. In what seemed to be less than 10 minutes, she had every board lined up where it should go. Since the bottom of each board fit six inches above the patio to prevent flooding from the pool getting into the house, each placement was brutal. I shanghaied a neighbor, and it was done, not only in time but just in time. But the storm kept moving south.

Miami was terrified. The famous Brickell Avenue office building canyon was block after block of glass skyscrapers and condos. If the storm hit Miami directly, coming in off the Bay, it would create a shrapnel storm, millions of shards of glass whipped around for miles, killing, maiming, and wounding anything in its path. But the storm kept going and finally hit south of the city in Cutler Ridge. Here are a few "highlights."

- People from where the storm was supposed to hit drove for hours to shelter in Miami. At least one was killed because of that misjudgment.

- Scalpers were selling bottles of water for 10 and 20 dollars a bottle. Many were arrested.
- The entire community of Country Walk was flattened. Hundreds of homes were destroyed.
- A news clip caught a construction dumpster, filled with debris, beginning to turn crazily in the wind. It straightened out and rolled right down a street. Viewers could watch it, like a torpedo, aimed straight for a house that it obliterated.
- There was a picture of a steel beam in the middle of someone's front door looking like a huge arrow shot from a bow.
- Unless one was intimately acquainted with the city from years and years of living there, it was impossible to find one's way. The winds removed all the street signs and any significant locators like large trees.
- My assistant director and his pregnant wife lived in the storm's path. They sheltered in an interior bathroom, as people are directed to do, brought a mattress with them, also as directed. As the house began to shudder and shake, he had his back against the wall, his feet pushing the mattress against the door—for over an hour! When it was over, he opened the door. The bathroom was about all of the house that survived. He was looking out at the street. His wife began to have contractions. He put her in their large SUV. Before they got to the street, the debris had flattened all his tires. A timely flyover by a Coast Guard helicopter saw them and sent an ambulance. She had miscarried by the time they got to a hospital.

With my hiring confirmed, we packed up and left Atlanta, a city with four distinct seasons, the two nicest being the longest, the two worst ones, the shortest, and arrived in this steam bath. At our far southwest Miami destination, I opened the door, stepped out of the car, and mosquitoes intent on sucking me dry descended upon me. We were so far west that we abutted the Everglades. From the Everglades, you get mosquitoes, snakes, and a particular toad called a Buffo toad that can weigh three pounds and is so poisonous that if grabbed by an unattended dog or cat, the animal can go into convulsions in minutes and die. And in the category of things not to forget, there are alligators.

A word about alligators: they are very deceptive. A mature alligator can run as fast as a racehorse for about 40 yards. An adult male will weigh as much as 600-800 lbs. and be 13 feet in length. Females are smaller, "only" 500 lbs., and about 9 feet long.

They are nasty, irritable creatures that eat anything they can catch, including dogs and children. Every year several children are snatched from a shoreline because they stood too close to the edge; most are killed or maimed for life. This very morning, December 20, 2022, a newspaper headline greeted me. The story told of a man at the edge of a lake, washing off grime from his hands. An alligator grabbed him by the arm. He escaped the beast with severe injury to his arm and only survived because he had the presence of mind to call 911 while fighting the creature and, then while waiting, create a makeshift tourniquet from an electrical cord. He has many surgeries before him and may lose his arm.

Running at 40 mph, this is the first part of the alligator that gets to you.

During mating season, alligators take over what they deem to be their world. I've seen traffic lined up for miles as game wardens and cops tried to dislodge a gator that ran for cover under a car.

Miami is famous for lizards: geckos, curly tails, and iguanas. There is a lizard called the "Jesus Lizard," When startled, it will race to the water, rise up on its hind legs, and run across the surface to safety. Would I lie about someone named Jesus? But the alligator is the king of the lizards, no ifs, ands, or buts. Odder still, everyone down here takes all this for granted.

Jesus Lizard: Lots of funny things to say including that there's a band with the same name. Oy!

●●●

Miami is also famous for Stone Crabs, but less well-known except to locals is the land crab migration. Stone crabs are delicious; most land crabs are inedible; some land crabs are poisonous. Stone crabs are beautiful. Land crabs look like blue/grey slate. Hundreds upon hundreds of them rise from the ground like locusts. The clacking sounds they make as they traverse the cement make you feel like you're watching the making of a horror movie. Their shells are so hard, they will shred your car's tires if you run over one.

Now we have pythons, courtesy of the dumbbells who bought them as pets, not knowing or believing how big and powerful they get. Some escape from their tanks, seek out body heat, and have strangled a child asleep in a crib or bed. Some just escape, while the owners release others into the Everglades, decimating the animal population. Here is something that happened which will stop you in your tracks. Rangers discovered an 18 ft. long python that had fought, killed, and swallowed a five-foot alligator—whole! That's not the kind of magic Miami wants visitors to think about. Yet to those who live here, "that's life."

BACK TO WORK

Shortly after I got settled, I received a phone call from one of the two men who controlled Jewish Miami. His name was Arthur Teitlebaum, of fairly blessed memory, the regional director of the Anti-Defamation League of the B'nai Brith. He was used to being the first call on all Jewish issues besides Israel. First and foremost was anything about antisemitism, the ADL's bread and butter. I met him at a lovely restaurant where many patrons, even the waiters, recognized him. He welcomed me. We sustained a cordial conversation, and he paid for lunch. Well, ADL did. As we got ready to depart, he said, "I wish you luck, but if you get in my way, I'll step on your head." With that, he left.

Teitlebaum had a big head start on me; he'd been in Miami for eight years. He was well-connected politically. He was the go-to guy for the press on anything that smelled of antisemitism. It wasn't long before I heard, "Did you hear what Teitlebaum said . . . ?" It was about me and summed up with this phrase: "No competition." Harumph! I had to find an end-around strategy. I would follow the wisdom of many guerrilla fighters: pick your battles.

I began by introducing myself to the press. My brother, with whom I was very close, was an icon in television news production. He had the magic touch of taking national TV news programs from third to first in the ratings. That meant huge increases in ad income. He was also well-known in the print media because of his many pungent articles about the news business and what it needed to do to survive in the coming electronic age. I could now get an equal shot at being on camera or in the newspaper. My last name was magic. I wanted producers to know me; they made the decisions on stories. I wanted hungry, young reporters to know me. They needed to establish themselves. Due to my brother's training, I was a good interview. I also learned, "Make your point, regardless of the question."

Next came the coalition building, my forte. I had come to Miami with an introductory letter from Atlanta's Archbishop to Archbishop Edward A. McCarthy of Miami. At that time, McCarthy's province covered the lower third of Florida, east to west coast, and up to Vero Beach. A power to be reckoned with, he didn't like my arch-nemesis Teitlebaum. I was now connected religiously to a vast area of Catholic territory. He met me graciously and willingly because, to mix a metaphor, I was stamped kosher by his brother archbishop.

The Miami Jewish population at that time was approximately 250,000, compared to Atlanta's 35,000. Luck played me a good hand. A key rabbi from Atlanta took a pulpit in Miami, so near the time for the transfer, we could have rented a van and moved together. We were good friends and able to help one another in our work. When some Catholic youths vandalized his synagogue, he called me, not ADL. In this incident, I saw a teaching lesson, so I went to the priest where the offenders' families worshipped. Remember, I was Catholic kosher. We made a deal. I would create a short course on Jews, Judaism, and antisemitism. The boys would attend in exchange for the rabbi not pressing charges. The icing on the cake was the press got wind of it and loved it. A *quinella!*

Cubans were the fastest-growing segment of the Miami population. There was also a small but very well-to-do Cuban Jewish population called "Jewbans." They, of course, were split between a cultural divide (old Jewish adage. "Two Jews, Three opinions"). Some had Sephardi roots (Spain and the Middle East), and most were Ashkenazi (Polish, German, Russian). Therefore, of course, each branch had its own synagogue. The other divide was geographic. Due to conditions in Latin America, Jews from numerous countries came to Miami: Colombians, Venezuelans, Mexicans, and natives of all the Central American countries. They were all different and had no use for each other. The Jewban country club almost went bankrupt because of a fight for control between the old-time Cuban leadership and new, on the make, Columbian Jews.

After the Mariel boat lift, the population jumped even higher and brought the dregs of Castro's jails and mental hospitals to the area. Crime stats jumped with the population. The first wave from Cuba, which arrived after the revolution, had done well. They were angered and embarrassed by the new refugees. Most of the refugees started on Miami Beach, where a large, elderly Jewish population became an easy target for criminals. I spoke more than passable Spanish. Trying to speak another's language, except in Paris, makes one *sympatico* (a feeling of warmth) to the listeners. To whit, I gave another perfectly awful half-hour speech in Spanish this time at a convention in Panama and got a standing ovation—for effort.

●●●

Two program prongs came from the boat lift. For the social welfare issues, I studied the factions and frictions among organizations claiming representation for Cubans. I chose one, The Cuban American National Council. We worked on a variety of projects for close to ten years.

The other trick would be finding a bridge between the right-wing post-revolution arrivals who, for vague reasons, tended to be anti-Semites. The answer? A monthly breakfast learning session called . . . hang on to your seat, folks . . . "Black Beans and Bagels." Cute—no? The attendees loved it. So did the press. I was making progress.

I said that Lady Luck had dealt me a good hand in the Jewish community. Every rabbi wants Jewish power brokers in their synagogue membership. Many made overtures. I chose the leading Reform Temple because it was close to the diversity of downtown and had a powerful sense of "*Tikkun Olam*" (repair the world), which was meaningful to me. They would join in a lot of my programming. Finally, I mentioned that the Atlanta Jewish population was tiny compared to Miami's. When AJC decided to move the regional office to Miami, the Israeli government saw the same arrow pointing south.

Israel's consulate general, headed by Ambassador Yoel Arnon, could have boarded the same caravan with the rabbi and me. Arnon and I became colleagues and friends. When the peace accords were signed between Sadat and Begin, he invited me to watch the historic event with him at the consulate. I was the only Jewish leader so honored. In like Flynn.

I'm not writing the Encyclopedia of Me, so bear with me for a few more pages while I hit several important career highlights: Then we'll be headed toward the finish line.

THAT'S WHY THEY CALL IT WORK

Social Club Discrimination

Miami was checkered with discrimination.

The most influential social committee in Miami politics was The Orange Bowl Committee. To them fell the organization of the hoopla that went with one of college football's premier post-season games. The Committee handled housing for the players, any amenities needed, the creation of the parade with its sale of tickets and seating arrangements, and infinitely more issues. To be seen as a Miamian who was a "someone," you tried to finagle your way onto that committee. Membership would give connections that ran to the top of Miami influencers. It was the crown jewel in the Miami political tiara. Its chairperson was Sister Jeanne O'Loughlin, president of Barry University. The power behind the throne was Alvah Chapman, publisher of the *Miami Herald*. Nothing got done in Miami that Mr. Chapman didn't approve of, or so it was said. It worked in reverse, too. If he wanted it to happen, it usually did.

I had been poking around the issue of country club discrimination. This was an issue for which I got roundly smacked in Atlanta. When Jimmy Carter became president, he named Griffin Bell, of Atlanta, as Attorney General. Everyone knew that he belonged to the Capital City (Lunch) Club, and everyone knew that club was restricted. Stupidly naïve, I wrote him a letter explaining how he could change the face of Atlanta discrimination by resigning from the club and denouncing discrimination. A week later, I got a call from the president of a

Speech in Panama to Fedeco.

powerful construction company. To put it bluntly, he threatened me. If I ever raised the issue again, I would be blackballed from Atlanta and fired from my job. With a wife, two babies, three dogs, and multiple car payments, I was in no position to be a hero. That lasted until Miami.

Miami was checkered with discrimination. There were high-end islands like Star and LaGorce where it was rumored that Jews, Blacks, and Latinos couldn't buy. There were country clubs that didn't and wouldn't have members of those groups. The ADL was pushing for a state remedy. They devised an ingenious idea concerning any club with boat docks. The legislature passed a bill that prevented boats from a discriminatory club from using its docks. Why? The water belonged to the state. Chalk one up for the home team.

I had the local approach. I got the Puerto Rican mayor of Miami, Maurice Ferrer, its first Latino mayor, to sign an order. It prevented any city department from spending money at discriminatory clubs. Using that model, I followed up with over a dozen surrounding cities, including Hialeah, Florida's fifth largest city, to do the same. I had manufactured a dozen or more news articles. I had put a sizable crimp in the pocketbooks of those who discriminated. I was a happy camper.

Then one day, reading about the coming Orange Bowl, I was . . . well . . . let me describe it this way. Back in the '40s and early '50s, comedians Goodman and Jane Ace hosted a popular morning radio show. Jane was a Gracie Allen type, prone to saying some very odd things. When something surprised her, she would explain her shock with, "Why you could have knocked me over with a fender!" That's what this print revelation did to me. A discriminatory club would be the site for the Orange Bowl postgame ball. Time for another letter. This time, I knew I was in the right stadium. University presidents are not in the same category as the Attorney General of the United States of America.

It was a simple, straightforward, informative letter. Was he aware that his players would be like Cinderella? Once the ball ended, none of his non-white players could go to that club again. I was being a good Samaritan. I thought he'd like to know before the press discovered it. 'Worked like a charm.' The ball was passed to a fancy hotel . . . Look in the dictionary for the definition of thrilled, and you will see my smiling face.

Nor was I done. As Jerry Reed sang, "When you're hot, you're hot . . ." I went to the paper's editor, Dick Capen, who was a hot shot in his own right, having been a cabinet officer for Richard Nixon. I pitched the story to him with a warning. "Your boss, Mr. Chapman, is a member of several of these clubs. This time the fender hit him. His reaction was, "Damn the torpedoes! Full steam ahead!" Two weeks later, the Sunday edition of the Miami Herald had a screaming headline about social club discrimination. Throughout Sunday, Monday, and Tuesday, their investigative reporters laid it all out, club by club, with tense, embarrassing interview after tense embarrassing interview.

Mr. Chapman rose to the occasion. He condemned the policies, resigned from some clubs, and hatched a plan to break down the restricted country club to which he belonged. There was back then an independent afternoon paper called the *Miami News*. Its publisher was Jewish. He was a brash stereotype of the gruff, cigar-chomping, rumpled-suited newspaperman portrayed in Hollywood and on TV, a step down from Lou Grant. Chapman asked this. "If I get the consent of the board's majority to accept you as a member, would you apply?" The pawn met him with reluctance. Not only do journalists not like to be the news, but he was also nothing like any other of the club's members in dress or demeanor. Were it not for the respect and power of Alvah Chapman, "no" would have been the answer. He applied.

As there are in many ointments, there was a fly in this one. The voting was by secret ballot, with the ballots immediately destroyed once counted. People could vote their hearts, and their two-facedness in lying to Chapman would never be known. The membership gambit failed. Chapman or no, the answer was no. It was another news story covered, if I recall, in both papers. The embarrassment was immense; I'm not sure his wound ever healed.

The Russians are coming!
The Russians are coming!

Alan Arkin wasn't there to make it funny.

Let's take a break from bigotry and take another peek at something personal. Sometimes, comes a day when nothing is planned, and nothing is happening. Then something unplanned happens. This was such a day. It was the height of the Soviet Jewry movement. The Miami Jewish Federation was a lead player. The logistics of such work are mind-boggling and take tremendous management skills and coordination. It is a multi-maze of details to fight one's way through to the end. There is federal paperwork. One has to find an accepting family that will take responsibility; relatives are the first choice. There is the learning of a new language. Housing has to be found, and the furnishing of it so that it isn't just a flat but has the semblance of a home. There has to be food. And the refugees have to be taught to navigate the everyday life skills we take for granted.

Here's an example. A newly arrived Russian woman is taken shopping in a supermarket. She is told to make a list, is picked up, and taken to the store. One of the things on her list is canned vegetables. They go to the canned foods section. Mind you, at home, in Mother Russia, she would be facing one shelf either nearly or totally empty. If a can was there, you took it, no questions asked. Here she was faced with double or triple shelves that ran the length of the store. The choices might have been: different cuts of beans, cans that had the same thing but were from different companies, low salt, cans of single or mixed vegetables . . . and the beat goes on. She became so overwhelmed that she had a panic attack and passed out in the aisle. She said later, "If I can't even buy food, how will I learn to live here?" True story.

My desk phone rings. It is someone from the Federation. "We've been looking at lists of people who have applied to get out. There's a Dr. and Mrs. Guralnik. That's pretty close to Gralnick. Could they be relatives?" Yes, they could have been. The records show they were from the same area where my family came from in Russia and a file photo of one of the grandparents was a dead ringer for my paternal grandfather. As they used to say in the '60s, "close enough for folk music." Yes, they could be relatives.

Next question. Would I sponsor them? I was divorced, had two youngsters, and was living in an apartment that shared a disturbing resemblance to the kinds of places the community found for the refugees. On the one hand, this was a *mitzvah*—doing a good deed— something central to Judaism. On the other hand, did I really know what I was getting into? The answer was no, but I said yes anyway.

The family was at the international transit point in Italy. They had the choice between Israel and America. They had family in Israel but decided to check out if the streets here were paved with gold. They also had relatives in Boston; it doesn't snow in Miami. So, it was settled. In a few weeks, Federation called with their arrival information. I bought myself a "learn it yourself" book on Russian phrases. I spoke passable French and Spanish. I had some Yiddish under my belt. Russian? Forgedaboudit! The Cyrillic alphabet? Greek to me. English would have to do.

While I had pictures of the family, this would be our first meeting. I waited with growing anxiety as people streamed into the reception area. How would I recognize them? It turns out finding a group of bedraggled, sleepless people looking like scared rabbits was pretty easy. There they were: two grandmothers, one grandfather, one father, one mother, a beautiful girl in her sub- teens, and her younger brother who had a scowl on his face that lasted about 25 years to his untimely death. We greeted and hugged. One of the grandmothers, who was the daughter and granddaughter of rabbis, began to cry as she hugged me and said something I would never forget, the kind of thing that instantly made me feel that I had made the right decision regardless of how it all would turn out. She looked me in the face, tears flowing down her cheeks, and said, "Villiam, you are my Moses." Digest that. It is a "wow" moment.

Off we went to baggage claim. Came a bag or two, then two or three more, then . . . until the number was twelve. Each was bigger than the last. Young brother was not into claiming baggage. Daddy and I did the heavy lifting. Did I say heavy? I grabbed the handle of one bag and felt like my shoulder had risen and my left forearm and hand remained attached to the bag. It was "you need a weightlifter for this" heavy. I exclaimed, "What the hell is in this thing?!?" The answer was pots and pans. Cast iron ones. The Russian authorities told them that such things in America were for the rich, so they brought their own. We managed to get everyone, and everything, outside to the taxi stand. It was one a.m. The air was as heavy as the suitcase. In minutes, everyone was covered in sweat. Boston, some thought, might have been the better choice. I had a bigger issue to deal with. We had seven adults, two almost adult-sized children, and twelve suitcases. I didn't need a taxi. I needed a Ford 350, which of course isn't a part of any taxi fleet. Had I any idea what I'd be facing, I would have rented something. As it was, not a taxi driver would look me in the eye. I finally hired three cabs, put the luggage in one, and divided the people amongst the others, and off we went.

The Federation had arranged rooms at a lower South Beach hotel on Miami Beach. As our Russian caravan pulled up, the doorman and bellhops decided it was time for their break. Gone with the wind. We checked in, got luggage carts, and headed for the elevator. It took several trips up to their two rooms. Seven people, 12 large suitcases—anyone remember the stateroom scene from the Marx Brothers' *A Night at the Opera?* It was about 3 a.m. We had an early morning appointment at Social Security. I needed some sleep and left them to their own devices, wondering on my return if I'd find a note that said, "Nice meeting you. If you ever get to Boston, let us know." But they were there. I had been given a stipend to get them through the first few days. We had breakfast for many and headed off to the SSA, me playing the Pied Piper and them in tow. It was just up the street from where we were. No more than 100 feet in our *schlep*, mother stopped, in shock. We were passing Woolworths. And what was on display in the window? Nice new shiny aluminum pots and pans. And on sale, yet.

We entered the Social Security Administration office, and I could see everyone tighten up. Being in a bureaucratic office in Russia was usually not a good place to be. After a short wait, a heavy-set black woman brought us to her desk. Another shock. I don't think they had ever seen a black person in their lives. Mother spoke the best English, so she did the paperwork. We only got to "last name" on the first form, before we hit a snag. They spelled their name Guralnik. Mine is spelled Gralnick. Family lore is that all the Gur's, Gra's, and Gro's were related. When the administrator began to write Gura . . . mama balked. "I want to spell my name like his!" That, of course, was a no-no and brought another lesson. Russian problems like that were solved with money. When mama asked me about that, I said, here you go to jail for paying off people. In Russia you go to jail if you don't pay off people. An hour later, the Gura's were signed up for Social Security and Supplemental Social Security. Within a month the elders would have a steady flow of income. This is a wonderful country.

Now we needed places to live. The Federation took care of that. Paternal grandpa wanted a separate space. They got him an efficiency. Maternal grandma wanted her own place. They found one for her. She was my "Moses" person. She called me after she saw the apartment. I thought a conversation would be almost impossible. It wasn't. She only needed one Yiddish word, and it was a word I understood. "Villiam," she said, *Schmutz! Schmutz!*" That means dirt. "*Schmutzik! Schmutzik!*" That means dirty. She was unhappy. I bought her cleaning supplies. The rest of the family, including the paternal grandma, found a place very central to the heart of South Beach. They were happy. Now we needed jobs. I quote this often: Al Cap's Pogo—"We have met the enemy, and he is us." The family began to become its own worst enemy.

POPPA'S STORY

Poppa was not a rolling stone—until later. Poppa was a dentist. That, one would think, is a good thing. He could go two hours up the road to the University of Florida Dental School, and in two years, he would be a licensed Florida dentist, and the family would be set and stable. But what about those streets paved with gold? Oy.

The beginning was doing illegal dentistry for other Russian immigrants using whatever tools he brought with him and jury-rigging some Black and Decker stuff. Then he found a job as a dental assistant. All the while, he was planning—and borrowing money. Like many immigrant groups in America, the Russians maintained a black market that included what was more or less loan-sharking. What did Poppa want the money for? Tractors. Somehow, he thought he could make a killing selling Russian tractors to Americans. Let's just say Miami isn't the Midwest, and the market for any kind of tractor isn't what it is out there. Then there were import regulations and fees and the need for places to store them and someone to sell them, etc. ad awful. The business failed. The money, however, was still owed.

Then came the nightclub. A vodka-soaked, good-looking women-stocked Russian nightclub, it would be. But there were problems. One was qualifying for a liquor license. Some questions aren't asked because the answers aren't what you want to hear. I just yelled and reasoned and argued and got nowhere. One result of the nightclub gambit was what I felt became alcoholism. With the frustrations of failure, the money owed to who knows who, the drinking increased. There were fights at home, late nights out, and then tragedy in what I assumed, and the police agreed, was suicide. Suicide by bus. Screaming down Biscayne Blvd, roaring drunk and way over the speed limit, he ran into the back of a bus. Why was it assumed to be suicide? Because there was no indication that he made any attempt to slow down or avoid hitting the bus. Now mom was on her own.

MOM'S STORY

Mom was the quarterback. She was an MD in Russia. She couldn't return to med school with two children and a spiraling downward husband. She became an esthetician. While her first studio primarily served Russians, her reputation grew. The studio was a success. She opened another. Husbanding the money, she was able to buy the family their first home, a condo. Making her own potions that were very well received, the sales of cosmetics increased her business and income. She bought a small property in North Carolina. It was quite a growth process to watch. I was more nervous about what she was doing than she was. Ultimately, she was able to buy her son an apartment. Then the death of her husband began the denouement. It all became too much for her. Again, came the moneylenders, the financial problems, and the business failures. First to go was the house in North Carolina. There was the need to sell the family apartment and move back into the rental market. It was hard to watch as she dealt with anger and depression.

And then there were the kids. The soon to be sensational-looking daughter had serious adjustment problems and quickly became anxiety-ridden and depressed. And the son continued to scowl while he went from an angry atheist to an orthodox Jew with various meditation-driven gambits in between. However, there were two happenings with brighter lights, one of which burned out like a glowing candle.

Some candles burn bright with promise. Others burn down the house. Momma had a serious relationship in Russia with her professor in medical school. He was not Jewish. Her family objected; his family objected. She ultimately married the dentist. A period of extreme antisemitism was probably the impetus for them to become Refusniks. When the dentist was at his nuttiest, momma flew back to Russia. She found and took up with her old flame. When Poppa died, she somehow got her professor into the United States. He spoke almost no English and had a terrible time learning it. America wasn't for him. He became depressed and, like any good Russian, turned to the Vodka bottle. He couldn't get a job in his field, which would have required a mastery of English and a wide technical scientific vocabulary to boot. He became a taxicab driver. Drinking and driving, we know, do not go well together. There were accidents, and in another mystery, he actually ran someone over and killed them. Yet the police ruled that he wasn't at fault.

Over time, he sank further and further into depression, drank more and more, and became a burden on Momma physically and financially. He fell ill and left her bereft. She moved, with the help of her daughter, to Miami. It was the same building that was their first owned condo, but there had been a drastic change in the neighborhood in the intervening twenty-plus years. Rarely did she venture out. No longer full of Russians, the building's primary languages were Creole and Spanish. She is today alive, unwell, has little dogs and cats, a car, actually a truck which won't go very far, and is trying to get money to move back to Boca Raton. You may be thinking that the daughter would step in again. That story is still to come.

The bright spot was their first Passover in America. Friends of mine invited me, my kids, and the Russians to their seder table. I told a friend at one of the TV stations, and it became the lead story on the 11 o'clock news. Again, the Moses thing and another experience that made me feel clean and wonderful inside, that I was doing a good thing. As I said, the candles' bright lights would turn short-term celebration into long-term catastrophe.

THE SON

I've previewed his story. We'll bring its end down to its essence. Was it an accident, as the family said? Or was it suicide, like the police said? He was out late at night, either walking off a drunk or just being drunk and walking. He was crossing a drawbridge and fell off. The impact of hitting the concrete below killed him. I was called on to find a rabbi and make arrangements for a funeral. Doing *mitzvahs* isn't always uplifting.

THE DAUGHTER

The children of Refusniks were given scholarships through the eighth grade at the Jewish Day School. The son and daughter did better and better. By graduation, they had a grasp of English, a grasp of how American kids their age dressed and what they did, and they got a grounding in their religion. Most Jews were so cut off from Judaism by the Russian government that they knew next to nothing about it. And, of course, they got a good education and were made ready for high school.

Around her sophomore year, the daughter turned into a stunningly beautiful young woman. She was tall, maturely filled out, with long blond hair and a sweet, alluring face. She had a portfolio of pictures made that had modeling written all over it. I urged her to take them to a reputable agency and see what they said. Shyness and insecurity kept that from happening. During this period came the loss of her father and maternal grandparents. More rabbis for me to find. There were the various moves, the coming and going of businesses. She became the family therapist dealing with whatever at the moment was causing her brother's scowl and her mother's tumult; life was becoming increasingly rocky. We spent a lot of time talking.

Memory fails when the big moment arrived.. Along came Jones, long, tall Jones. Except his name wasn't Jones, and he wasn't all that tall. What he was, was a catch. He was born in Russia and came here with his Refusnik parents as a young child. Thus, unlike my family members, he was thoroughly American Michael, Michael though not being his name. He was an accountant with a bent for business. They met, they courted, I found a rabbi, they got married. She was a radiant bride, but her radiance didn't hide her neurosis. As she was dressing, something went wrong with the dress. She had a total meltdown, weeping and wailing, sitting on the floor in the radiant dress, and declaring she couldn't do it. She did. If you can survive the drinking,

Russian weddings are a lot of fun. We all did, and they began a fairy-tale life.

Accounting got to be a bore. Suddenly came an idea born with close Russian friends and contemporaries. They opened a restaurant that featured healthy foods. It was in a toney neighborhood where being fit was everything. The restaurant was jammed for breakfast, lunch, and dinner. The patrons were so loyal eating was like eating with family. Everyone knew everyone. The husband and wife, along with their friends, ran a good business, so good they decided to expand. On a personal note, the husband could gentle his wife; they prioritized active vacations and quickie jaunts. They were skiers, and he was a mountain biker. They were healthy, happy, and expanded the family while they expanded the business. Two girls were their offspring. The restauranteurs became the financial cushion for everyone else.

The first move was for the daughter to open a mini version of the restaurant but in a very big mall. It did well, but they had their eyes on bigger things. It is here we must pause for a moment of reflection. Sometimes in life, there are warning signs. They are big, they are in flashing neon, and they are right in front of our noses. Yet sometimes we miss them. That is what happened. This sign said, "DO NOT DO BUSINESS WITH RUSSIANS!" They saw what happened to Poppa. They saw how Russian moneylenders were ripping off their fellow immigrants. They saw a Russian underground that could be, and at times, was dangerous. While their parents would have had difficulty getting loans from banks, they certainly would not. Nor would they have had trouble attracting creditable business partners. Russians were the choice. Here's what happened.

They decided to try franchising. They found a Russian in Boca who opened the first gambit. In sum, he ignored the franchise agreement, stopped paying the fees, but still operated under the business's name. There was hootin' and hollerin' and lawyers, but they were doing well enough to say 'the hell with it' and look elsewhere. Elsewhere would be New York.

If you can make it there, you can make it anywhere. They couldn't. After searching for the perfect location and gearing up for the shock of the real estate market in the Big Apple, they found a place and began construction. They had a grand opening. They also had a flood. Here's the short story. Storms hit the city, it rained torrentially for days, and the basement filled with water. Maybe, they could have had the first health food store with the swimming pool, but unfortunately, the basement was full of more than water. It was full of their stock, their machinery, and their supplies. The city condemned the building. Now they were out of a bunch of money. But hope springs eternal.

Back to Miami they went. The neighborhood that had the best match for their first success was at the upper end of Miami Beach. There, they seemed to hit their stride. The daughter who had great artistic ability did a free-hand, wall-size mural in the restaurant and chalkboard daily menus. The place was a hit from day one. Then I got an odd call. They wanted to exchange vows to mark their coming anniversary, would I marry them at the restaurant? I have no authority or certification to do that, but she said, "we're already married, so there's nothing legal needed, please just work something up." The ceremony was one of the strangest things I've ever done. I worked hard on it. 'turned out that didn't much matter. Russians are eaters and drinkers. They are not listeners. There were times I couldn't even hear myself. But oh well. The kids were happy, so I was happy.

With this restaurant, the four friends decided to incorporate. A board of directors was formed. I still can't figure out how what happened did. They now had extra investors and another set of hands and minds. Sometime after the wedding and the realization that this place was going to be a smash hit, the two best friends, the people who with daughter and husband were inseparable, vacationed together, raised their kids together, made a cabal with other board members. They walked in and announced they had held a meeting. They outvoted daughter and husband. They could stay and work if they wanted but were voted off the board. They lost their financial interest; all that remained was to fight over the financial settlement. Years later, I believe that fight is still going on.

While things were going so well, they found a house on Miami Beach. Old Miami, it was built out of cement and concrete and wreaked charm. They put a fortune into it. Now it's sold. But one of the daughters is in college, doing well, and seems to have found a better version of her grandfather. The other, an amazing dance talent, is exploring the field of dance, working at it for incredible hours a week, and shows professional promise. So those are good things and a good ending.

You must be frustrated as to why there are no names. As they say in *Dragnet*, . . . to protect the innocent. Why not make them up? Why? I thought this worked just as well and hope you do too.

The end here is another reflection. If there is a moral to this saga, I don't know what the hell it is. What did Sinatra croon? "That's life."

Tragahdiah is Yiddish for tragedy written phonetically. It doesn't only mean tragedy. Like so many words in Yiddish it has varying usages. When someone is about to tell a story that has opera-like complexities, they might say, "Listen to this tragadia." Why, you might ask, is this Jewish tragedy in a book about work?

For most people, work is not confined to a bubble or a space capsule. Work becomes the center of the rest of life's merry-go-round. What is on the merry-go-round impacts work; work impacts being able to deal with the merry-go-round. To write a book about work and leave out life doesn't tell the whole story. This, as several other entries, is why I've written it in rather than left it out.

The Klan—Again

As I pulled up, my heart was beating like a snare drum.

Now to deal with something that was important in a different way—the Klan.

Fighting the Klan was an adventure that followed me from Atlanta to Miami. Upon arriving in Miami, my exploits with Jerry Thompson and his book, *My Life in the Klan*, where I was called the best Klan watcher in the country, followed me. That anointing was a gross exaggeration, but who am I to argue . . . ? We were to meet in Sarasota on Florida's Gulf Coast. I took Route 27 instead of Alligator Alley. It ran through "old Florida." Populated with old Florida types—lots of farms, lots of trucks. The suburbs of Miami this was not. The traffic stopped and then began to crawl. In about 10 minutes, I came upon a scene from a bad movie.

In front of me were several robed Klansmen on both sides of the road. They were holding buckets to collect donations. (Bring me that fender again, please . . .) As I pulled up, my heart was beating like a snare drum; I was sweating as if I'd just run the 440 in the summertime heat. No, I would not donate, but . . . But would they try to pull me over? Would they try to intimidate me or intimidate me more than I already was? There's a big difference between researching and writing about extremist groups and coming face to face with them. I also knew that the local constabulary must have condoned this activity, or the Klansmen wouldn't have been able to block traffic. Having kept my windows raised as I approached them, they waved me on. I breathed a great sigh of relief.

This odd scene was a prelude to another. The local Klan decided to put down roots in Miami. They received a permit to rally in front of the Courthouse. Assembling on the courthouse steps one sunny day, they got the crap kicked out of them. (A note: there is no Ku Klux Klan. There are many around the country, some affiliated, some independent, some moderately extreme, some very.)

And so came and went the Klan in Miami, but antisemitism remains.

It is essential to know what antisemitism is and what it is not. If you don't, this can happen. There was a very popular, expensive French restaurant in the Aventura area, a high-end community just north of Miami's city limits. If you are a fan of Jackie Mason, you are familiar with his routine about how Jews act in restaurants. Here are a few of his lines. On being seated near the kitchen—"is this a seat for someone like me?" Receiving a plate of food: "The portions, the portions, what happened to the portions?" A general observation: "To a gentile, they are thankful they are being served." Suffice it to say that area of Miami, heavily Jewish, had many folks that fit Mason's stereotypes. A patron argued with the waiter over the size of a portion. He insisted on seeing the manager, who did not resolve the problem to the customer's satisfaction. Next, he wanted the owner. The argument got very loud and very heated. Finally, the owner asked the patron to leave. He did.

Calling the owner an anti-Semite as he walked out the door, the man hatched a plan for revenge. He was, as many condo dwellers are known, a "condo commando." He had his sphere of influence, was politically active both in the condo and the area and would bring that to bear in his plan. He made the supposed antisemitism of the restaurant owner a happy hour subject of conversation. He also posted flyers in his building and adjacent ones urging people not to eat at a restaurant owned by a Jew hater. It worked. The restaurant came close to bankruptcy. Here's why definitions and actions are important. The owner sued for liable. He won big-time.

Kissimmee, Florida

Two simple words—centuries of complex problems.

While we are on antisemitism, let's run up to the Orlando area and visit with the folks at a high school in Kissimmee, Fl. New to the area, I thought the town's name was pronounced KISS' a-me. As I paid the toll, I asked for directions in one word, "KISS a-me? And she said, "I will if you want, but I think what you really want is Kiss-SIM-mee. Make a left."

Humor is wonderful. What I was there for was not.

City Seal: Pucker up.

Church and State

The alphabet can be confusing.

One of the difficulties in learning English is that it has many words that look and sound alike but are different. That was the case in Kissimmee. The local high school football team wasn't doing great; the student body wasn't helping. There was little school support. The administration came up with "Spirit Day." The Friday before each Saturday game, students were tasked with making posters, designing T-shirts, and coming up with anything fun and supportive. There would be a Spirit Day rally as well. So far, so good.

For those of you who are Christian or who have studied Christianity, you know that spirit has a religious connotation as in Holy Spirit. A group of Christian teachers planned a sneak attack to capture the "spirit" concept. They were faculty advisors to the Christian student's club. To them, Friday would be a salute to the Holy Spirit and all his/her/its cut-buddies. Suddenly on Fridays, students at school began to sport T-shirts with messages from Mathew, Luke, and other apostles. There were signs and posters galore and a prayer meeting. All knew a separation of Church-State fight loomed. To them you could practice any kind of Christianity you wanted. What to do? What to do? I had a brainstorm. I would call and make an appointment to see the Chairperson of the School Board and the school's principal. That's what brought me to the toll booth and my pronunciation lesson.

To say the meeting was short would be an understatement. To call its tone curt would only be close. To say the participants were hostile and aggressive would be accurate. I couldn't count fast enough the variations of "who do you think you are's?" "mind your own businesses," and "this ain't no south Florida county full of New Yorkers." "There's the door" was an easy conclusion to draw. I don't remember an invitation to return or even a warning not to let the door hit me on the way out.

I wasn't done. You need a complainant, lawyer, and judge to find something a violation of the law. We found a Jewish teacher who was very disturbed about what was happening. He agreed to file a suit. We brought in the ACLU. Now we had a complaint, a bunch of amicus briefs, and began to prepare for trial. Amid preparations, the complainant didn't show up. He had resigned from his position and left the state. We also heard later that his peers had isolated him and subjected him to wicked antisemitism. "He who runs away . . . ?" I don't know, but he took the case with him. No complainant, no case. I went back to South Florida, called New York with palm trees, and assumed that, decades later, the Holy Ghost still holds sway in Kis-SIM'-mee, Florida.

Race Riots

. . . the man hatched a plan for revenge

The years I was in Miami were probably the tensest in its modern history, save for the Cuban Missile Crisis. There were two race riots, one I had box seats to from my office window. I could see the clouds of black smoke rising towards the sky. I watched curls of smoke rise from buildings and emergency vehicles racing to them.

Another awful time was the early outbreak of AIDS. Fake news didn't start with Donald Trump. Rumors started that the disease began in Africa and was brought to Haiti. Haitians, it was said, brought it to Miami as they went back and forth to visit family or migrated to South Florida. Within weeks the thousands of service jobs in South Florida held by Haitians were devoid of Haitians. Short of being herded into detention centers, the community could not have been more isolated or set upon. It was terrible. Finally, science came to the rescue, but it took time for science to be believed. Sound familiar? The fact that Haitians spoke Creole, were black, and came from a country settled by African slaves stoked the fires.

View of Haitian landscape, Hispaniola.

149

The Leo Frank Story

CONTINUED

"What would you say if I told you I could prove Leo Frank was innocent?" I was on the next plane.

Leo Frank: Without the rope around his neck.

Being in the intergroup relations business during this period meant long hours, watching your back, and meetings severely taxing one's nerves. I needed a break. I had met a young woman in Cleveland. I was there for a speech. She was very exotic looking, and we shared a passion for baseball. An AJC member, she and I crossed paths several times during that year. Recently divorced,

I was living in a three-room, not a three-bedroom apartment in which I put a set of bunk beds for my sons. As Jerry Reed shouted, "She got the mine, and I got the shaft!"

A second story walk up, the apartment's bedroom faced the window of an apartment whose resident was Cuban and who was a domino fanatic. Every weekend he had the "*caballeros*" over for beer and dominos. I didn't know there was yelling in dominos. The clicking of the tiles remains firmly fixed in my brain.

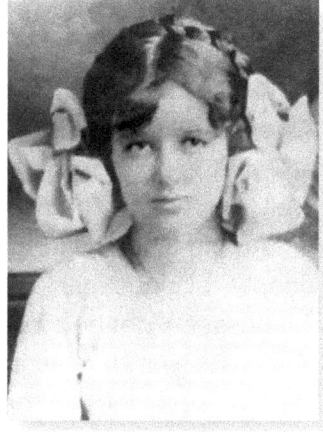

L'il Mary Phagan, as she was referred to.

The clicks and clacks, sounding like toy false teeth, jumped out the window and echoed against the outside walls before jumping through my windows. There's no sleeping in dominoes, whether you're a player or a bystander.

For heating—and cooling—I had a window air-conditioner which gave off neither much heating nor cooling. We had a very cold winter; that used to happen in South Florida. I ended up with pneumonia.

Scheduled to go to Israel to lead a multi-generation family mission, I was told by the doctor to "Forgedaboudit!" He too a transplant from Brooklyn. I said dying in Jerusalem was a *mitzvah*, and I was going. I didn't die but I thought I was going to. About every ten years, Jerusalem has a snowstorm. Yup, you guessed it. If it weren't for bad luck, I'd have no luck at all.

The apartment gave me another lasting memory. One day, I came home from work and had one of those "what's wrong with this picture?" moments. I had been robbed. Seven of my adored antique clocks had been stolen in broad daylight.

To boost my spirits, I called Cleveland and shortly had company. I can't say it turned out to be like the Connecticut experience, but we didn't click for some reason. The last time, you will recall, I was saved by a pseudo-call from the police chief. This time it was Jerry

Thompson, and for real. He was in North Carolina and roaring drunk. "What would you say if I told you I could prove that Leo Frank (Leo Frank, murdered by the Klan, was the only Jew ever hanged in America) was innocent?" I answered, "the only thing you could prove at 2 a.m. is that you couldn't get up from whatever you're sitting on." Well, it turns out he had the goods.

An old-timer in North Carolina had read Jerry's Leo Frank story. A deeply religious man, the caller was on his deathbed. He called the Tennessean, got hold of Jerry, and Jerry was with him in a day's time. 'turns out that he was in the pencil factory the night of the murder. He had seen the janitor carry Mary Phagan's body to the elevator shaft and drop it in. He told his mother, and his mother told him, himself a teen, that he had to go to his grave with that knowledge or someone might kill him. Having accepted Christ in his life, he couldn't die without exonerating Leo Frank lest he end up in hell. Jerry said to me, "How soon can you get your ass to Nashville?" My date, lying next to me, was listening raptly to the conversation. What she didn't expect was my answer to Thompson. "Now!" I was on the phone finding her a flight home and me one to Nashville. She and I never saw each other again. It speaks well to my failures in the single world. That would change seven years later and a few pages down.

To reinforce the point, let me add how the heavens can hint that a relationship wouldn't work out. I met a girl from Kansas City at one of our national meetings. She was pretty, but more than that had an energy about her, a great personality. Unlike so many AJC members who were lawyers and academics, this young woman was a businesswoman. She owned a string of fast-food restaurants and was on her way to becoming wealthy.

During a break in the meeting, we went for a walk. Washington, DC is right up there with any city for romantic walks. We walked from the hotel down to the Mall. We sat on a bench facing the Lincoln Memorial Reflecting Pool with Lincoln to our right, Jefferson in front of us, and the Congress to our left. It was a wonderful May day. As we talked, we both began to lean. Shortly we were shoulder to shoulder, her head on mine. What could go wrong? I'll tell you. At the moment, between the head on the shoulder and the coming kiss, a bird needing a bathroom dropped a load. It hit me on the back of my head and slid, warm and wet, down my neck coming to rest somewhere along my spine. I took it as a hint. She helped clean me up, which was mortifying. I didn't think I could deal with a relationship that had this incident as the answer to the question, "So, how did you meet?

Having done with the heavens, let's get back to our reporter who found the gold pot at the end of his historical rainbow. Jerry came to Atlanta for a meeting I arranged with the key Jewish professional leadership. He convinced everyone he did have the goods. His timing was impeccable. For some time, there had been discussions about clearing Frank's name. Now we had it. What we needed was a strategy for its use. There was an additional problem, how to get around the protocol involved. It is, shall we say, bad form for an out-of-market newspaper to come into another market and do a major story. Seigenthaler didn't care. It was decided that our target was the legislature. We wanted a pardon or exoneration. To get that, we had to divide and conquer.

We needed agreement from the Phagan family and the Frank family. Several important Jewish community members were state or local legislators, politically well-connected. They would draft a bill and, in its introduction, both families' feelings could be presented. There was a prominent state legislator who was a branch on the Phagan tree. One of my most powerful AJC members and a giant in Atlanta construction and leasing was related to the Franks. And then came the discovery of the diamond in this historical mine, Mary Phagan. Mary Phagan was a direct relation to our dead child in the basement of the pencil factory. Assignments were handed out. Mary Phagan was handed to me. This would be a doozy.

"Girl left her family and is not heard from for years. She finally calls from an Indian Reservation to tell her mom she's marrying a Jewish Indian. "Really, mom. His name is Whitefish ..."

– Old Jewish joke

"Better the kingmaker than the king."

– Machiavelli

Jim Conley

Factory "Super" and Real Murderer

Mary's great-grandniece, Mary Phagan Kean, has written a book, *The Murder of Little Mary Phagan*, where she details her research into the case. It's incredible that someone can compile that much information and still think Frank is guilty. She also discredits Alonzo Mann's deathbed confession from 1982 with little more evidence than "because I said so," so I guess her insistence of Frank's guilt shouldn't come as any real surprise.

It wasn't hard to find her. In those days there were such things known as telephone directories . . . Mary Phagan lived in Marietta, Georgia, a suburb of Atlanta, a very conservative suburb. Newt Gingrich was a college professor in the area, and its congressman was a member of the John Birch Society.

Other than calling her, I don't remember what I said to get an appointment. I must have said I was a reporter, and we were working on a story about "little Mary Phagan," as she was known. Could she help me with my research? Before the enormous growth of metro Atlanta from in-migration, almost everyone from Atlanta sounded like they were from the south. A sweet, lilting voice answered the phone. Had there been Facetime, I would have bet there was a bourbon and branch water next to the phone. Yes, she would be happy to help.

I don't know what I was expecting, but what I got spun my head around. Another hit me with a fender moment. Mary Phagan was a teacher. She was not married. She lived in a large, lovely home—lots of wood, glass, and stone. She was in her early to mid-thirties. To ask a woman her age was a major no-no in the South. She was a pretty woman and very easy to talk to. She greeted me at the door and led me through a hallway into the great room with a large, working fireplace. She offered me a seat and seated herself in front of the fireplace. The head-spinning came next. Above the mantel was an almost life-sized painting of her namesake. The girl in the painting and the woman seated beneath it could have been mother and daughter, they looked so much alike. This was not going to be easy.

I made my pitch. Not an emotional one. As Sgt. Friday used to say on *Dragnet*: "Just the facts . . ." She listened intently, waited politely, and didn't even fidget. There was a look of sadness on her face. Then it was her turn. She addressed me formally making her comments the same way I made mine. She was sad for Leo Frank and his family. Yes, she had heard that "Mr. Frank" might not be guilty. The key word she said was family. "Mr. Gralnick, I might be inclined to agree to your request, even if it would stir up a hornet's nest. But you see, my daddy believes with all his heart that Leo Frank murdered our family member. I hope you understand, but I can't go against my daddy while he's still alive."

We said a solemn goodbye. She thanked me and I thanked her. I made a report to the group. Only the Jewish agencies wanted to proceed. Seigenthaler was with us. Onward we would go. We ended up getting half a loaf. We wouldn't be able to get the votes. The appeal shifted to the Georgia Board of Pardons and Paroles. In 1986, they pardoned Leo Frank. He was never exonerated. I was drained, but it felt good, nonetheless.

The Papal Visit

I'm the only Jewish person you'll meet who had a Saint involved in his marriage.

A mere Pope until death—then a saint.

●●●

Let us finish with another "biggee," a huge event no matter where it happens. This time it was happening in Miami—a papal visit. Complicated such a visit always is. But this was Miami. It turned out to be seven-layer cake complicated. The Pope is a spiritual leader of about one billion people. He is also the head of the Vatican State, a city-state of a few thousand people. A pope is often involved in geo-political issues. That was the case with Pope John Paul XXIII.

157

He had decided to meet with former Nazi and then current Austrian President, Kurt Waldheim. The Vatican received communications of condemnation from nearly every Jewish organization in existence. Included was one from Miami. The archbishop also heard many anti-Catholic, threatening comments as well.

Next complication. The Pope was an ardent adherent of the Second Vatican Council's principles on ending antisemitism in the church and fostering Catholic-Jewish relations. There are significant, important, influential Jewish organizations in every large city in America, sometimes four-five-or six of them. The Pope wanted to meet with the Jewish community but had not the time, desire, or strength to have a gaggle of such meetings, which in themselves are very tightly scripted affairs. You think an invitation to the Prince's Ball that Cinderella went to was a sought-after invite? 'Nothin' compared to a Jewish leader wanting to be in the room with the Pope. The list would be small because of security concerns and the Pope's desire to create a sense of intimacy. Drawing it up was brutal. A pre-meeting dinner for about 50 people, hosted by Johannes Willebrands, the Cardinal responsible for Jewish-Christian relations, would solve some of the problems. For many in that room, it would be as close to the Pope as they'd get.

The archbishop had appointed me as an arrangements committee member. It was an exciting but unenviable task. Remember, Miami had large populations from Central and South American countries, all of whom were titularly Catholic. An outdoor mass would handle their needs on Sunday. Somehow, through good management and good luck, we were prepared. Then lightning struck. A rabbi in Miami with whom the archbishop had a long relationship read him the riot act over the Waldheim meeting. That was the last straw. He recommended to the Vatican that the meeting with the Jews in Miami be canceled and moved to New York, or just canceled. It was a "we'll show them!" move. While the awaited answer from the Vatican had everyone having their pacemakers checked, the archbishop held some peace negotiations. A joint statement hammered out by both sides made everyone's points in diplomatic terms. The event would go on. After the pre-papal meeting dinner, the next day would be THE day. It is important to point out that many archdiocesan figures and area priests wanted the meeting canceled. Criticizing the Pope, they felt, in such terms, was a step too far. One of them became the current Archbishop of Miami.

Through the work I put in, and the relationship of trust I'd built with the archbishop, I was invited to the dinner and the meeting. The setting was fancy, and the hotel food was passable. The value of attending was for one's ego and one's resume. Willebrands, who spoke with a very heavy Dutch accent, was near impossible to understand, and the acoustics were awful, but the speech was scripted, and we got copies.

Those attending dinner and the morning meeting checked into the Omni Hotel at five o'clock in the afternoon before the Papal meeting. Not 4:59 or 5:01. Once in the assigned rooms, we could not leave them until escorted to dinner. After dinner, I went back to the room. I noted every sleeping room had a law enforcement person stationed in front of it equipped to fight a battle. I said to the person in front of my door, "Do I have anything to worry about?" His reply? "If everyone on this floor left every door to every room wide open, the only thing you'd have to worry about is flies." Ok. Got it.

Breakfast was room service. At 8:30 a.m. we were escorted to the other side of the hotel and seated in a large conference room. It was full.

The motorcade stands out. It was the same as for a head of state. Several cars in front and in back of the "Pope-mobile" protected it. An agent told me there was enough weaponry and ammunition to hold off an attack from a small army. There was air protection as well.

Another interesting side note produced a sound bite that became a piece of history. After the event, the Jewish community held a press conference run by an eminent American rabbi Mordechai Waxman. Waxman spoke glowingly of the reconciliation the Pope was trying to build. No, he was not an anti-Semite was Waxman's opinion. While displeased over the Waldheim meeting, the Jews had to understand that the Pope was head of state and head of the church. "Was Waxman satisfied?" the press asked. "Yes!" The questions continued. The reporters kept pushing him on the meeting with Kurt Waldheim and issues between Israel and the Vatican. Was Waxman still satisfied? More likely, he was just aggravated. He turned to the questioner and responded, "You know, sometimes you just have to accept yes as the answer." I've used that line countless times. Had there been social media, it would have gone viral.

The icing on my cake came a month before the Pope's arrival. That is where the beginning of the end of my bachelorhood began. My mentor in Atlanta, Rabbi Emmanuel Feldman, said that it was an honor whenever one spoke from the *bima* (pulpit). He should build the talk around the weekly Torah portion. I got pretty good at it, learned a lot, and I spoke at many Shabbat services. I received an invitation from a new rabbi in Boca Raton, the leader of a prominent conservative congregation in South Florida, B'nai Torah. He was kind enough to invite my boys and me to dinner. There I met his girlfriend, Andrea. Baltimore, which historically had deep AJC roots and a strong Jewish community, was her home. Conversation was easy and lively. She was attentive to my boys without being overbearing. The fact that she had an electric smile didn't hurt much.

At the end of dinner, the rabbi rushed us out the door and left Andrea behind to clean up and do the dishes, like it was expected. If it caused her to be late, so be it. The rabbi went to the garage for his car. My sons, Justin, and Marc, walked with me out the front door to get ours. As we stepped outside, a girl with very long legs, very short pants, and not much of a top rode by on a bicycle. She waved and yelled, "Tell Rabbi Ted hello from me." Of course, who she was, we had no idea. My oldest, however, turned to me, and with all the wisdom of a teen said, "Dad, something is goin' on here, and it isn't good." Out of the mouth of babes . . . He was right. That was the girl the rabbi was *schtupping* on the side. We get to *shul*, as does Andrea. I am sitting on the *bima* (raised area containing the pulpit, the arc and the torahs) with the clergy; Andrea is seated in the congregation with my sons. Now comes God's first intervention.

My topic was the anniversary of the liberation of a death camp for children, *Terezin*. The Nazis often used the camp as a prop for Red Cross visits. There was a children's orchestra, a chorus, etc. The children told the truth about what the camp was doing to them as they died from malnutrition and disease by writing poems they stuffed in cracks in the bunks, holes in the pathetically thin mattresses, and into the joints of the bunk beds. Scholars created a book with the children's works titled *I Never Saw Another Butterfly*. The volume is almost as thin as its authors. But reading it leaves a heaviness in the heart and an uplifting sense of pride in their courage. I urge you to read it.

It turns out that Andrea had produced a community play based on the book. She felt she was the only one in the synagogue, and I was talking only to her.

Had a match been struck? You'd think so, no? It had, but it blew out a few times. We chatted for several minutes and continued on the phone. I had a speaking engagement in Boca, and she attended. We chatted some more. She asked me what kind of girl I was looking for. How much broader a hint could I have come up with than this? "Someone just like you." The answer should have just been, "you." So, she fixed me up with her girlfriend. Ba da boom. After that date, the girl, Jewish, told Andrea I was too Jewish for her. Where's Jackie Mason when you need him? Now came God's second intervention.

In preparation for the Papal visit, the archbishop asked me to think of a few projects that would bring needed knowledge to the Jewish community. One idea was to do an interview on Jewish TV called "Everything You Ever Wanted to Know About Catholicism but Were Afraid to Ask." That was when Haim Ginott's book about parenting was the rage. The second mini brainstorm I had was holding a meeting for Jewish professionals at the Jewish Federation. It would be the same topic but would instead be a lecture. The real brainstorm? Invite Andrea, the acting director of the Community

Jewish Day School. The topic and what it would impart would have no relevance for her, but I thought it would test her willingness to drive 50 miles during rush hour to see me do my thing. She did.

When I got the RSVP, I began to plan. I am an active lecturer. I walk the room or stage if the layout makes it possible. It keeps people alert. I wrote a note, "I'm interested if you're interested." I figured during my wandering, I'd slyly drop it on her desk. How adolescent is that?

The room was filled. She took a seat. My lecture began. About 15 minutes into it, God or Thor decided to put on a show. There were booms of thunder that shook the building and lightning flashes that turned night into day. The rain came down, well . . . , like it rains in the tropics. Suddenly, the lights went out, the emergency lights went on, and an electronic voice began to intone, **"You have five minutes to exit the building. You have five minutes to exit the building."** Outside was a hurricane-like storm, the kind where umbrellas are of no use, and the rain soaks one to the skin in seconds. That happened about two feet from the exit. Welcome to the subtropics. I rushed to catch her, shoved the note in her hand, and sloshed my way to my car. By the time I got home, she had telephoned (remember the "brick" phone?). Her message was, "I'm interested. It's your move." God would have one more go with us.

To show you how suave I was, or su-wave, as we said in Brooklyn while trying to be suave, I asked this single-parent, working woman out on a weeknight. I would offer her a full night. Drinks, dinner, and a movie. By the way, I thought courtesy required that I ask the rabbi. Even though they had broken up, he had the gall to be very snippy about it.

I dressed in my sharpest new casual outfit (which she later told me made her think that if this was my taste, maybe I wasn't for her!), and then the phone rang. She had to cancel. The arrest of a teacher in her school for child molestation was headline news, and she didn't want to be out and about.

I was having none of it. The date would be therapeutic, I counseled. She reluctantly agreed but told me to pick up a paper on the way. When I saw the headline and read the story, again I got cold blood. The molested child was a girl. Her daughter went to that same school and was seven. O—M—G! Again, I was too blockheaded to assume that if it had been her daughter that I would never have been able to persuade her to go out.

How did it go? This woman can get high if she gets too close to a bottle of alcohol. One drink, and she's tipsy. After two drinks, she needs support. That night she had two stiff drinks. They had the impact of two glasses of water. She is also afraid of her shadow. The movie I chose was *Psycho*. Came the famous shower scene, it was I who shot up out of my seat like someone had touched me with a cattle prod. I thought I needed a defibrillator. Andrea, the fearful, sat there like there was nothing on the screen. I took her home.

We had a few dates before the papal visit was upon us. Things were going nicely. Now we go back to the morning of the papal visit. As the archbishop walked the pope down the aisle, he would stop to introduce certain people to his Holiness. I wasn't expecting one to be me. I was wrong. God's more gentle hand was at work. I've met many important people through work, including several presidents. This was like no experience I had ever had.

There's an old joke about the garment district worker whose 50th anniversary is coming up. His co-workers chipped in and bought the couple a trip to Rome and, through political contacts, arranged for him an audience with the Pope. When he returned to work, everyone gathered around. "So, what kind of fellow is the Pope?" they asked. His answer? "A 34 regular." Another ba da boom. My description of him is different.

Surreal? An out-of-body experience? As the archbishop turned the Pope towards me, I became aware that I was breathing. That is not natural if one is healthy, which I was. The archbishop's introduction of me to the Pope contained very kind things. The protocol is you don't touch the pope or extend your hand unless he does. He did.

As we shook hands, he took mine in both of his. They were soft, gentle hands. It felt like a father's comforting touch on his child's head. Suddenly, the room was empty. He and I were the only ones there. The bright lights dimmed into a heavenly haze. I told him I was thinking about getting married. He said, "I know you are Jewish. Do you mind if I pray for you?" "I'd be honored," was my response. He blessed me with no mention of Jesus, only the Heavenly Father. Then it was over. The people reappeared; the lights went up. The Pope was the nicest 34 regular I had ever met.

Andrea and I became engaged a few months later. I needed those blessings because I do things that on reflection make me scratch my head. I read an article about other cultures and marital engagements. The egg was central to them, something from which came life. I decided I would give her a gift-wrapped egg, not a Faberge egg, but one from a chicken. Our engagement dinner took place at one of Boca's five-star restaurants, the *Vieux Maison*. The name is perfect. It was a historic house turned into a restaurant. I learned later that Andrea was expecting me to ask her to get married, which was my intention. She didn't understand why so many courses came and went with no ask.

After dessert, I finally popped the question and gave her a box with imprinted hearts and an egg inside. It was easy to tell it was not a box that had held a ring, which was what she was expecting. Way too big. She was non-plussed. I had to explain. She said yes, and I yelled, "She said yes!" Patrons and staff applauded. She wanted to rush right home to tell her parents, who were sitting for her daughter, Amanda. I'll leave it to you to play out her mother's reaction. There was no ring, and there was that egg to explain. Now Andrea wanted to tell her daughter. I urged her not to wake the child from a deep sleep and have her try to digest this. I was right. "Oh no! You promised you'd never leave me" was followed by weeping and wailing that lasted well into the night. Sometimes women should listen to men . . .

And so ended the night of the engagement. We got married by the side of a designer pool, in which floated candles and lotus blossoms, in a friend's designer house. We had made a rule. No one was to be invited whom we would be meeting for the first time. My mother-in-law was not happy. We had a one-night honeymoon in a hotel on a lake, some 2 ½ hours away. By the time we arrived, Andrea had been asleep for two hours. But thirty-three years later, the box is still in the refrigerator. We've never opened it. Lord knows what that egg turned into. I do know it didn't turn into a chicken, at least not yet.

BACK TO WORK ONCE MORE

One of the things a skilled director of an organization does is bring in new members and develop new leadership. As Willy S. said, "There lies the rub." A couple was recommended to me by a board member. They had a Coral Gables address (that's good), were in their late 40's (also good), were financially above average (so-so), progressive on civic issues (another good thing), and he had a lust for a seat on the Board of Governors (always good). The hard part of the equation was that he had some peculiar ideas, like my having been director long enough. Hmmm (very bad).

After a few years and his ascendancy to the board, he offered this: "Bill, what's the next step in your career?" I told him I had taken it and was perfectly happy where I was. His reply: "Don't you think you've done this long enough and that we should have some fresh blood in your chair?" I began to think that maybe I needed some fresh blood in his chair. It was threatening. Having gotten to know him reasonably well, I knew he was like a terrier with a bone, just not as noisy. He continued, "You're a talented guy and good for Miami. Give me the heads up, and I can get you a better job in several area non-profits from which you can choose." It pretty much floored me (where's that fender . . . ?). While I had the votes, so to speak, I'd seen this happen to other colleagues and knew working in an environment where someone was constantly gunning for you was not a professional's definition of fun. It turns out once again that timing is everything.

*"Stories aren't made of language:
they're made of something else . . .
perhaps they're made of life."*

— **Philip Pullman,** *Daemon Voices:
On Stories and Storytelling*

*"Don't tell me the moon is shining;
show me the glint of light on
broken glass."*

— Anton Chekhov

Book Four

The AJC Years—"Rat's Mouth," Palm Beach County

"If you buy that Rolls Royce, don't complain to me about the cost of insurance."

– AJC member's wife

"If a captain wanted to keep his boat safe, he'd never take it out of the water."

– St. Thomas Aquinas

Boca Raton

Nothing ratty about this place.

Anyone with a rudimentary knowledge of Spanish knows Boca Raton means, "mouth of the rat" or "rat's mouth." But no one can tell you for sure why it's called that. The most common explanation is that a Spanish explorer saw this potential debarkation point on the map. The shape of the land mass and how it opened into what we know as the inter-coastal waterway that would protect the ship looked like a rat's mouth. Let's leave it at that.

Boca Raton residents are so enamored with living here that to them it's always just Boca, not Boca Raton. On his first exposure to the town, my youngest, seeing Boca this and Boca that said, "Well it's real easy to remember where you are in this place." Another out of the mouth of babes moment . . .

I was responsible for Palm Beach County from Miami and cultivated the chairman of that non-resident professional chapter.

To visitors, the seal has the full name;
to us'ns, it's always "Boca."

WILLIAM A. GRALNICK

He hailed from New Jersey. He was an AJC president and Board of Governors member who had moved to Boca Raton. He wanted the chapter in Boca to have its own director. After all, Palm Beach County had 1.1 million people and at this writing was 17% Jewish. Once his donation hit a million dollars, he was a voice with which to be reckoned.

At the same time, another leader stepped forward. He was a developer and entrepreneur (he had a toy company that gave the world the Cabbage Patch Doll!) from Connecticut who moved to and ultimately bought a high-end, West Palm, gated community. Not just into—he bought the whole thing! He wanted more say in AJC and a more professional presence in the unmanned chapter. He became another member of the million-dollar club.

They also had in common that they wanted li'l ole winemaker me transferred to Palm Beach County. The timing could not have been better. The boss asked me. Andrea was already there. I had big money behind me. While I loved Miami, I would have the Jewish professional playing field in Palm Beach County to myself, no one giving me heavy competition, I'd again be a big fish, and Boca seemed to be a neat pond in which to be. I said yes. Flags didn't line the streets, but I was cordially welcomed and got to work.

First, I had to find an office central to my leaders' locations, but that cost as little as possible since the move happened during the middle of the budget year. A local philanthropist who was not involved in AJC, but was a close friend of my New Jersey supporter, came to my rescue. He owned a building on Federal Highway, central to downtown office buildings. He had 450 square feet of unusable space and said if I could make it an office, I could have it rent-free.

It was a peculiar design. On entering, you were in a little bulge of space. Perfect for the secretary/receptionist. The space then turned right, where there was a support column for the whole building. Behind the column, the area ballooned again and had windows. Perfect for me. However, unless I wanted to film a deodorant commercial, I wouldn't be holding any meetings. I did, however, have several members, businessmen, and lawyers nearby whose offices had large board rooms offered to me for board meetings. I was ready to roll. The following year we were in the budget, and our landlord gave us a proper office, configured properly. Now I could have one or two people in, but for several reasons, continuing to use classy boardrooms appealed to everyone, including me, and made us look more substantial than we were.

The American Jewish Committee is, by charter, a lay-run organization. Our job as professionals was, in theory, to train members to replace us. They would write letters to the editors, be interviewed on the news, frame and lead the programming. That's the way it worked in Atlanta. That's the way it pretty much worked in Miami. That is not at all the way it worked in Boca. We had a board discussion on the matter. In the middle of it, my gated community owner said, "Enough of this. That's why we have you!" End of discussion. Truth be told, it was fine with me. Here's a truism. The fewer people involved in a decision, the faster it gets made. As it is said, "A camel is a horse made by a committee." With that decision made, we would accomplish significant things. (more foreshadowing . . .).

But quirkiness followed me. My 25th anniversary with AJC was coming up. The chapter threw a very successful fundraising dinner in my honor. I had two surprises. I didn't expect a gift, but before dinner, I was handed a voucher for an all-expense paid stay in the Bahamas for Andrea and me.

The other came as I was "working the room." I passed a table where sat a very famous rabbi and his wife. She looked very uncomfortable, eyes furtively looking left and right. She was hunched over. I thought I'd see if I could be of some help. As I turned towards their table, this is what I saw. A dinner plate with a large slice of prime rib being lifted from the table and tipped toward her open pocketbook. The pocketbook had one of those large-size plastic storage bags in it. Once the plate got to the right angle, in slid the food and closed snapped the pocketbook. Then she looked perfectly comfortable. May I again ask for the fender?

In those days, the Miami Beach days of Wolfie's and the Rascal House, such things were routine. Here is the playbook. If it was edible and uneaten, or sometimes just not nailed to the table, the customer took it home. Some old-timers would drop the rolls and muffins in a bag and then claim they hadn't been served any or wanted more. To some, who needed salt or pepper, what was in the shaker was about right so . . . Since no one either said anything or was anyone ever arrested, I guess management chalked it up to the price of doing business. While roast beef in the pocketbook was new to me, I saw it as an extension of the Wolfie's customer playbook.

I had barely settled in when the first community relations crisis hit. Unlike Palm Beach, Boca was "new money." Old money folks have a patrician way about them. You'd never catch one of them voicing racist or anti-Semitic tropes unless they were in their living rooms or "the club." New money folks? Not so much. It was not uncommon for a year-rounder to get into a loud squabble with a New York snowbird—about whom the one doing the yelling assumed was a Jew. The fights were often about a parking space (the population of Boca increases by 30-35% during the winter months) or the New Yorker acting or driving like one. You see a parking place; you accelerate into it. Someone else eying it? "TS." That's New York. The epithets would fly. Jew Bastard! Go home to Jew-town, and other pleasantries flew out of car windows. The snowbird's response? Usually, "F . . . U . . . !" That, too, is New York.

In those days, Boca had its own daily newspaper, the *Boca Raton News*, for which I wrote a weekly column. It had hired a young reporter who wanted to make a name for himself. He had a not-so-bright idea—an article about Boca-ites. He blended things like flip-flops with cotton balls on them, food snatching as previously described, and little old ladies who couldn't see over the steering wheel unless seated on a phone book or pillow. For good measure, he threw in the social rage of the day, women dying their tiny five-pound fluffy dogs the same color as they dyed their hair.

The intent was humor. As my speech professor told me in college, "humor is great—if your audience thinks it's funny. If they don't, you're dead." Well, his audience didn't think it was funny. To them, it screamed antisemitism. There's an old saying that only an n-word person can call another n-word person the n-word. So, it is with Jews. Jews will lacerate themselves with stereotypes as does Jackie Mason, and howl with laughter. A gentile does it, and holy hell breaks out.

I met with the owner of the paper. If he didn't want the paper's subscriptions to tank, think hard about firing him. He was—fired that is. I felt bad. There are some things about writing they don't teach you in journalism school; you must learn them in the trenches. He hadn't had enough trench warfare to see the IED on which he was about to step. The fact that his editor didn't stop the article in its tracks was inexcusable. He learned his lesson but also ultimately kept his job. No one said life was fair. Ironically, I thought it was a very funny piece, just one that shouldn't have been published in the local paper.

Jews for Jesus

The Jews for Jesus, in my opinion, were kids who manufactured
some mélange of Christianity that kept parts of Judaism so
their mothers wouldn't commit suicide. —William A. Gralnick

Next crisis: the coming of the Jews for Jesus, the largest of several Messianic Jewish groups. Scholars and religionists have written tomes about this the Messianic movement. Let me give you the cliff notes. You can't be a Jewish-Christian, the core concepts are antithetical. While Jesus and the apostles were all Jews, they set out to change Judaism. The Jews didn't want to be changed. The Jews for Jesus, in my opinion, were kids who manufactured some mélange of Christianity that kept parts of Judaism so their mothers wouldn't commit suicide. Old joke: Son comes home to tell his mother he's marrying a gentile girl. He asks mom if she'll be all right with that. Her answer: "Oh, I'll be fine. I'm just going into the kitchen, put my head in the oven, and turn on the gas." Think now for a moment about the meaning of the words New Testament. To have a new something, there had to be an old one to be replaced. Get it?

To be a Christian, you must believe in the Apostles' Creed. The creed contradicts the basic tenets of Judaism. Here you go:

Jesus, the son of God, was born in a virgin birth to his mother Mary.

He was crucified.

On the 3rd day, he rose to heaven to sit at the right hand of God the Father.

In Judaism, there is no division of the Godhead, there is only God. The rest is not Judaism.

When the Jews rejected Jesus and the apostles, you then had two different religions. There's no way to get around that—except if you are a self-proclaimed Messianic Jew. Here's an example. I headed the chaplaincy at the sheriff's department, I had an applicant who applied with the title of rabbi. His ordination, however, was from a Methodist Seminary. I couldn't hire him. To me, it was *chutzpah (being nervy)*.

Headquartered in New York, the Jews for Jesus, led by the former Jew, Moishe Rosen, declared a year of conversion. They would target cities with large Jewish populations and chose to start in Palm Beach County, a county that at the time was now 19% Jewish. To blunt their efforts, I needed to form a Jewish-Christian coalition, one from which would come denunciation of this scalp-hunting. The problem was many of the pastors didn't understand what the problem was. To them, it was just another form of witnessing. So, with a colleague, we chose six pastors and six rabbis and held monthly meetings. The rabbis would teach Judaism to the pastors, who would question the rabbis. It was some of the most meaningful work of my career. In six months, still six months before the Messianics were to hit town, we had our coalition and rolled out statements to the press and public.

In their first assault, they mailed out one million copies of the Christian Bible and Mel Gibson's odious movie about Jesus. Turnabout being fair play, many Jews dropped them off at churches, and many others attached a wrapped brick to the package and marked it return to sender. The recipient had to pay the postage and all of them had to figure out what to do with hundreds, if not thousands, of these returns. Everyone was singing, "Return to sender . . . address unknown."

Then came the march. Currently, marches, unless violent, aren't much noticed. In those days, it was a different story. This one was notably different because of its organization. Several organizations that served Jewish youth organized them to turn out. Large numbers of Jewish adolescents with placards faced older Jews for Jesus Christian adults, separated by police. It was a proud moment, one of those things as a Jew that gave me hope for the continuation of our people.

Every cloud has a silver lining, or so they say. Not true. Some have dark linings. One of the pastors who was part of the pre-Jews for Jesus rabbi-pastor meetings became a friend. He seemed like he wanted someone to whom he could talk. It turned out he did, but he led such a conservative church that he couldn't talk about the things he wanted to talk about with other pastors or congregants.

His denomination forbade divorce. His wife was sinking into mental illness. More and more often, she became violent. They had three young children, and he feared for their safety. He spoke to his superiors, who said a divorce would bring ex-communication. He'd not only lose his pulpit but could not belong to any church in the denomination. After a particularly violent episode, he acted like a responsible parent, moved out with the children, and sued for divorce. Almost instantaneously, he had no job, no friends, and no income. The dark lining eventually lightened up. He and the children moved out of state. He became a successful insurance agent and, hopefully, lived happily ever after.

There comes a time when a person begins to feel like a hamster on a wheel. I'd done about everything there was to do in my field. I didn't feel like I could get a better job without uprooting my family. Each move with AJC was more manageable than starting with a new organization because I already knew the ropes. With a new job, I'd not only have to learn the people, places, and things of it, I'd have to learn the ins and outs, facts and figures, things written and things unwritten. The latter you only learned if someone took you under their wing. The other way was the easier way. You made a mistake, and someone pulled you aside and told you what you'd done. I chose to stay, but I also had to re-frame my job.

It is good being 1200 miles from the mainframe, especially now that I had 25 years under my belt. I was respected and trusted. I knew I could do more things I wanted to do and fewer things that my colleagues in other offices were doing. Every few years, I would come up with a thread that would stretch for a few years. The chapter was running on autopilot, they saw my new adventures as bringing *kuvod* (strength) to the chapter, and if the money was coming in, I got away with it. A lot of it had to do with Israel.

My first gambit was easy. AJC, through its "Project Interchange," took non-Jewish opinion molders to Israel. The trips included meetings with the Israeli military, citizens, politicians, and a cross-section of the Muslim and Druze communities. One of the trips would be for journalists. With my contacts and familiarity with the news business, who better..? I cemented the deal by getting an up-and-coming news anchor in our market, Liz Quirantes, to be part of the trip. She had one caveat. I had to find someone in Israel from Palm Beach County who could do a series of interviews. God intervenes again, but of course—this is the Holy Land.

A friend's son had just moved to Jerusalem to study in a Yeshiva. I set up three encounters. How sweet it is!

Project Interchange: Journalists from near and far.

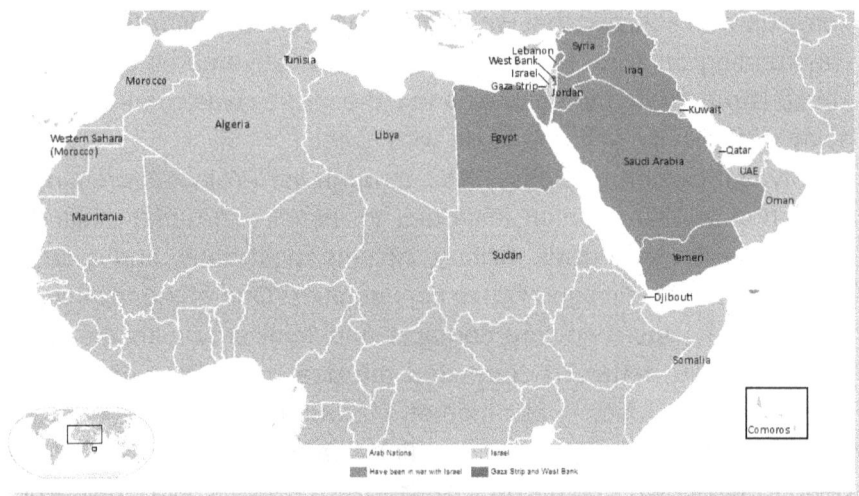

Israel: See that little line below Syria and between Jordan and Egypt? That's the whole country and why it's called a bad neighborhood for Jews.

●●●

The trip included a popular journalist from the Black media who was an arch conservative.

I also snagged the publisher of the *Miami Herald* and his adult son. We had a Korean journalist, a South American journalist, and a few American journalists who were non-Jews chosen by my AJC colleagues from their chapter cities. It became one of the most educating experiences I'd ever had. The biggest kick was seeing some of my tripmates post-trip nationally and locally on news broadcasts. The media covered it in both Israel and America as well as in the hometown presses of the participants. Many wrote about it in their home markets.

9/11 brought another first. Together a series of happenstance occurrences turned into a seven-year project. AJC had invited a command unit of high-level Israeli national law enforcement officers, including the Deputy Superintendent of the National Police, the #2 cop in the nation. Israel does not have city police with separate commands as we do. The national police create local commands.

The benefit is not having to deal with different jurisdictional commands during an emergency. A decision is made nationally, and officers moved accordingly. The purpose of the trip was to learn from Americans and American law enforcement officers about law enforcement in a democracy.

The schedule had them visiting a half dozen cities. None of my colleagues saw the mission the way I did. They booked the visitors into synagogues, arranged meetings with lay leaders and donors, and met political leadership. They arranged very few opportunities to interact with cops. The Israelis were angry. The biggest issue was the food. These officers had high military ranks; they ate in officer's quarters. They felt bagels on the run for breakfast and paper-wrapped Subway sandwiches for lunch were humiliating. The general was fit to be tied. The crashes at the twin towers heightened all these tensions. The general said the trip's focus needed to be changed; the Israelis should be teaching American cops about counterterrorism; yet nothing changed on their stops. A warning came from a colleague that I was about to receive a very unhappy crew.

After a hello and a handshake at the airport, the general jumped down my throat. He ripped me a new one and said one more sandwich, and he was pulling up stakes. There's only one thing one says to an angry general. It's "Yes, sir!" Soon, however, things would turn my way. First, I was honest. I said a fancy lunch was waiting for them, but sandwiches would be the centerpiece. Those would be the last sandwiches they'd eat under my direction. I made all my arrangements through the sheriff, a former marine, instead of local chiefs of police. His is the 12th largest sheriff's office in the nation. The largest municipal department topped out at about 160 sworn personnel. The Sheriff's Office? Twelve hundred plus, plus, plus. The sheriff detailed a friend of mine, then commander of the SWAT team, to set things up. The SWAT team handled dignitary visits. Waiting at the airport for these tired, irritated cops was a small train of highly polished black SUVs. The front and rear cars had enough ammo to fight off ISIS. They had as good as the Pope had.

It was military precision, lights, and sirens to headquarters. Now we were cookin'. Their first meeting of the three-day stay was about terrorism and given at a meeting to which the sheriff had invited all the chiefs of police and sheriffs in a three-county area plus any personnel of theirs to whom they felt the meeting would be relevant. The presenters received a standing ovation, and the sheriff presented them with medals. They met with the bomb squad and worked with the SWAT team at the gun range. The team practiced assault training in the buildings, along with their American counterparts.

There they met their first alligators. Our guys with guns drawn stood guard as the Israelis, armed with cameras, got insanely close to these beasts. Yes, they spoke at a synagogue, lunched with leadership (no sandwiches), and wanted to try some non-American/non-Israeli food. I gave them choices. They chose Mexican. What a night we had. One officer who was in the border patrol took this gigantic, circular Mexican hat off the wall to wear. I have a great picture of him. Three years later, he was shot dead by a Hamas infiltrator.

At the end of the three days, the general pulled me aside and said, "We can't teach you about counterterrorism. We must show you. You need to bring your people to us." I discovered that each American police department could apply to the Department of Homeland Security (DHS) for a grant that pays for counterterrorism trips. I arranged six trips. Since my contact for each trip was my general, Brig. General Uri Bar-Lev, I was granted fly-on-the-wall status in each meeting with Israel police or military. I learned a textbook's worth of practical and technical knowledge about counterterrorism. For us, the most important meeting was with the Bomb Squad in Tel Aviv, where, at a seaside bar that a few years prior had been attacked by guerrilla-filled boats, we had beer (a lot) and talked about the ins and outs of being faced with bomb situations.

There was a marker on a ceiling beam where an attacker's head ended up after being hit by an explosive charge. Our Lt., who ran our bomb squad, was so impressed with his new colleagues that he did a night tour followed by a full day. They showed us their brand-new, state-of-the-art bomb disposal truck. The sheriff's office was in the early stages of plans to replace ours. The Israelis gave us their blueprints. Its twin brother rolls in the streets of Palm Beach County. It was another wow in my professional story. A boy grows into a man, but there's always a little boy left within.

I have to take you back to Miami to finish the other Israel adventures, back to Key Biscayne Presbyterian Church, President Nixon's winter vacation church. The Pastor, Steven Brown, introduced me to an Armenian family. I was about to descend into a rabbit hole from which I almost didn't get out. I thought the poppa bear was the type to be everyone's grandfather. He was engaging, gentle, kind, generous (when he divorced his wife, he bought her a house on the same block as he lived so she could be near her children), and profoundly religious. What could be wrong? You'll see.

The father had, as a boy, witnessed the Armenian genocide. He was sitting on a train with his mother. Being on the train probably saved their lives. The family settled in Switzerland, where the now-grown man founded an extremely successful school. He had seven children, two homes in Switzerland, a compound on the Pacific Coast of Victoria, Canada, and a house on the tony La Gorce Island, Miami Beach. No one I knew had any idea where he got all that money, and as close as we became, I was never privy to that information.

People have different measures used to assess whether someone is trustworthy. Early in our relationship, I was leading an AJC trip to Israel. He mentioned that he had his first wife buried in the Armenian section of the old city, which had an Armenian church and cemetery. He had paid for perpetual care. Would I be able to find the time to visit it? I did. I was shocked. As I approached the church, the priest came up to greet me. I explained my mission to him and asked him to please let me see the grave. I don't know how one says perpetual care in Armenian, but this was more like perpetual uncare.

As I approached the grave, I had to argue with a large, wild goat for passage. Along with weeds around the headstone that seemed older than me, there were stones, twigs, and branchlets. The dirt hadn't been swept or removed in forever. The icing on the grave, so to speak, was the goat's droppings. They are, for comparison, much larger than bird droppings. I took pictures, and I took the priest to task. I gave him a fist full of money and told him to get this place up to snuff—and to keep it that way because we'd be checking. When I returned with the story and picture, poppa called the family together. I was unofficially inducted as an auxiliary family member. This was a rite of passage very few were allowed to make. On the other side of that door was a secret passage. We were in an enclosed room—family members only, and me. After I entered, I began to feel like Alice, and I couldn't find my way out. There was fervent praying and speaking in tongues. One of the sons and I developed a brotherly relationship. He had seen this cult-like seduction before. In a brief moment in a hallway corner, he warned me. About what? Keep reading. The relationship changes.

A contract was forthcoming. It would give me a hike in pay, but it would mean leaving a secure, rewarding position where most of what I did I did with no intervention. My new brother/protector sidled up to me and said, "Don't sign it." Then he disappeared into one of the mansion's many passageways. Sometimes, I listen. I took his advice. And so ended being the Jewish bolt in a deeply Christian nut.

Despite the mysteriousness, it was a great ride. Everywhere we went was first class, all expenses paid. I spent three weeks in Israel for Jewish-Christian meetings and helping with the advance work for a massive free public organ concert in one of Jerusalem's oldest and most famous churches. I had dinner with Billy Graham's daughter, who was married to the oldest of the family's boys. Speaking in tongues, *glossolalia*, was always mysterious to me. I experienced it more than once. For the uninitiated, one reaches such a fever pitch in prayer that the Holy Ghost envelopes the body. The Holy Spirit begins to speak through the worshippers. Words of no semblance to the mother tongue are the result. Very spooky.

We sponsored a conference at their Pacific Ocean home, many acres of ground overlooking the ocean. The jump-off to that were meetings in San Francisco. The Fairmont Hotel was our home base. It was the first time I'd ever had my laundry done in a hotel. I blanched at the charges. There came a warning sign that I sensed but didn't realize the meaning of until later.

I had an afternoon off and went to the museum. I pondered a painting while standing next to a beautiful Iranian woman. We got to talking. She was a psychiatrist. We walked and schmoozed. She asked me to have dinner with her; I readily accepted. I returned to the hotel to change and gussy up. Questions came about where I was going. The response to my answer was it would be frowned upon. What a chump I was; now I knew. Like a spy, someone in the family would oversee my every thought or action. It got worse. When I called to break the date, I found my beautiful Iranian psychiatrist meant dinner would be home-cooked at her apartment. Dinner was in various stages of ready and waiting for me, as was the implied promise of a sweet dessert. I felt like a heel for how I treated her.

After a few years, Pastor Brown moved on. There was a split in the family. One of the women married, two moved to Vancouver permanently, and one went off on her own into charity work. She became sort of a grifter. The younger son moved to Switzerland, becoming involved in race cars and bad company. My "brother" in the family had a severe falling out with his charity worker sister, with whom I had also become friends. I had to make a choice and chose him. Poppa died after a brief illness. I went to the funeral. One of his nephews conducted the service. He was on the way to becoming a major name in evangelical circles until he confessed his many sins. I think he left his church and moved to Texas to start a small church and rehabilitate himself. My family brother married and moved to Norway with his wife and newborn child. And that's the end of that story. Meanwhile, Pastor Brown and I continued our relationship.

Several times, I was invited to speak at Key Biscayne Presbyterian Church. Unlike the church in North Carolina, the congregants knew me or knew of me. They were proud of their Jewish theological roots and wanted to learn more. The church was in the round, which I found a difficult way to give a lecture, but I got the hang of it. The first time I spoke, I clearly remember the feeling of the house lights going down, the stage lights going up, and the house going silent. I happened to look up, and there directly over my head was Jesus, looking suspended in the air, hanging from a wire so thin it was almost invisible. I commented that it was nice to have company. 'nothing like humor . . . when it works. Again, I hit the bell.

For about a year, Pastor Brown did a traveling show. It was a Christianized version of Prairie Home Companion. What a hoot. Had he the backing, it was ready for prime time; it was that good. He was a nationally known teacher and preacher taught at the Hobe Sound Bible College and lectured widely. Whenever a church in the area invited him to do a teaching, I would go. "Folksy" was his style, but by the end, serious became his purpose. People were drawn to him like butterflies to nectar. I had a sense of pride that this was my friend. Listening to his lilting baritone, I often mused that if God had a voice it would sound like Steve's.

Liberal/conservative debate shows were the rage. One was *Point/ Counterpoint*. Steve and I did a few living room programs where we would argue the same points from our differing perspectives. It was fun and revealing. After each one, we ended up better friends than before we started.

When he moved from Miami to Orlando, he started a radio ministry, Key Life Ministries. On occasion, I'd drive up, do the show, and we'd have dinner together—two friends who agreed on very little but who enjoyed each other immensely.

He invited me to attend a weekend Christmas "party" (read "retreat"). I had my doubts. He read my mind. "No one is going to try to convert you," he laughed. What did happen was that some of the women there thought I was a perfect match for a winsome young member of Steve's ministry. She was cute as a button and a great conversationalist. Warning bells went off in my head; I listened to them. The rest I enjoyed.

I mentioned that I had dinner with Billy Graham's daughter, Gigi, and the family's oldest son. Going to a Graham worship service was an obsession of mine. Steve said if I insisted on going, he'd take me. As mentioned, I had met Graham before. He was my "assignment at a national meeting. My job was to meet him as he entered the hotel, escort him to the green room, and keep him company. As soon as our eyes met, the evangelizing power of Billy Graham came into focus. When his steely blue eyes locked on you, they felt magnetic, like you couldn't break the contact. And he hadn't said a word yet.

A Graham event is a textbook in organizational management. For weeks, maybe a few months before an event, the Graham team begins with the press getting the word out about the coming revival. There were visits to church pastors for the same reason. This is a broad net and cast carefully. The audience is warmed up long before there is anywhere to go. On the day of the event, the site is like a beehive of busy people. Critical is placing people from different denominations ready to talk to anyone with questions. If a person makes an alter call information is taken and sent to a prospective church for outreach. It is a well-oiled machine.

He had his eye on all of us.

At first, my encounter made me understand the power of this man. The lyrics of Neil Diamond's "Brother Love's Travelling Salvation Show" sprang into my head. Graham was tall and striking. This is what I heard in my head:

Room gets suddenly still
And when you'd almost bet
You could hear yourself sweat, he walks in

. . . Eyes black as coal
And when he lifts his face
Every ear in the place is on him

. . . Starting soft and slow
Like a small earthquake
And when he lets go
Half the valley shakes

. . . It's love, Brother Love say
Brother Love's Travelling Salvation Show

It was easy to see why everyone would . . .

Pack up the babies
And grab the old ladies
And everyone goes
'Cause everyone knows
'Bout Brother Love's show

On the other hand, he was by no means garrulous. Just as one describes a certain type of ball player with the phrase he plays country hardball, I would describe Billy Graham as a country preacher. He cast no electricity in the green room. He chatted with a few folks. The issue of Israel and the PLO came up. With no guile at all, he said that in a war, he'd bet on the Jews. Why? "Who would bet on camels when they are up against Mercedes?" At that point, I reminded everyone that whatever one hears in the green room stays in the green room. It was a startlingly un-PC comment from a man who had immediate access to America's power elite, including presidents. The Billy Graham who was chatting with us was not the Billy Graham who preached to over 60,000 people at Yankee Stadium. It was a heartfelt pro-Israel, pro-Jewish talk, devoid of Jesus, with no soaring rhetoric. He spoke from the heart, but he was a little nervous. This wasn't everyday material for him. Few non-Christians, fewer Jews, ever get to see two sides of the famous. That's what marked this as another happening I didn't think I would have had in almost any other job.

Israelis practicing a breech with PBSO SWAT team.

Book Five

Law Enforcement and the "I Didn't Quite Make It to Retirement" Job

*"I've got all the money I'll ever need,
if I die by four o'clock."*

— Henny Youngman, legendary
one-liner comedian

*"I always wanted to be somebody,
but now I realize I should
have been more specific."*

— Lily Tomlin, comedian, *Laugh-In*
star, movie and television
actress

THAT'S WHY THEY CALL IT WORK

If I quoted *Winnie the Pooh*, "And so we come to the end of it," I'd have to say, "fake out!" Fate would create a set of circumstances that included addictions, social services, a lawsuit, and a baby. Life was turned upside down by an experience that I call the best and worst decision of my life. Here's the short of it.

●●●

I had just settled into a happy retirement when a call came from a relative. He was in an addiction program, met a partner, and sired a child. The court sealed much of the information, so we'll call the baby "The Bundle." Trying with their heart and soul to pass the state requirements, they still had to give up their infant. The call was to ask if we would take the baby. We assumed that it would be for weeks. Wrong. A baby born in Florida has to be fostered by a Florida relative. We were it. We became court-appointed custodians until adoption. The judge ordered me back to work. He said, "Don't fall in love with this child. It isn't yours." I guess he felt being at work would keep that from happening. Wrong again. Ever seen a three-month-old child you didn't fall in love with?

The next day my wife called. The baby would arrive in a few hours. The social worker called. She would be there in 30 minutes not several hours. To the door came a woman holding a basket. In the basket was a baby, some paperwork, and some formula. This part of Florida is lousy with storks, and that's what this delivery brought to mind. She had been delivered by a human stork. Now you know why, "The Bundle."

You know the craziness that happens when people know they have nine months to prepare for a child? For us, 30 minutes was all we got. Not enough formula, no diapers, no crib, no baby blanket, no anything. One story will sum it up.

I drove to Target and bought a crib. I don't remember if the crib came with a mattress, or if I didn't have room for both in the car. I raced home, dragged the boxes of crib parts into the house, turned around, and raced back. Mind you, we had until nightfall to assemble this turkey. I ran into the store like a man possessed, had a quick conversation with a salesperson about baby mattresses, bought one, and manhandled it to the car. The car was a station wagon, and the mattress was longer than the car bed. It was a big car with heavy doors. I figured if I put down the back door on the mattress, the door would hold it in place. Wrong again, Ringo. The Keystone Cops should introduce the next scene.

Coming out of Target, I had to make a right and go up to the next intersection, making a U-turn to head home. I did that and stopped at the light after making my turn. I'm in a hurry. The light turns green, so what do I do? I floor it. Behind me is this whooshing noise. I look in my rearview mirror to see my mattress on the pavement. The traffic is too heavy for me to stop. I would have to go about one-quarter mile to the next intersection, come back past Target, make that turn again, and pick up the mattress. At that point, a car pulled into the road, two people jumped out, grabbed my mattress, and were gone in a flash. I'll be damned. What did I do? 'go back to the intersection and back to Target.

The saleswoman looked at me like she'd seen an apparition. I didn't even explain. What I did do is not take chances. They tied the back door shut, and this time I made it home with a mattress for the crib.

Those kinds of stories filled the next three days. Now, I needed a job, and the art of job hunting had become a science. I was still at the letter, resume, envelope, and stamp stage.

After a few misses and a few rejections, I turned to my former supervisor. She said, "You already know who is going to give you a job. All you need to do is figure out who it is." The Israel light went on nice and bright. I went to the sheriff and "poof," I was a civilian with the equivalent rank of lieutenant. I had three assignments: Homeland Security, creating and running a foundation, and re-creating and running a Chaplaincy. The business-Sheriff's Office partnership I created called BPAT (Business Partners Against Terrorism) became a Homeland Security Department "recommended" program. The chaplaincy became a model copied by other departments around the country. To do the "pitch" materials for the foundation, I did a profile of almost two dozen units that needed unbudgeted materials. Oh, the stories I could tell you, but then . . . I'd have to shoot you, so let's stop here. Ok, let's not.

Here are a few things I can tell you. The first is from Miami. I was on a ride-a-long when over the radio came an "officer needs assistance" call. We weren't in the neighborhood, but in those days, at such a time everyone drops everything and races towards their brother in distress. My guy floored the cruiser. We took off like a shot. The clipboard resting on the dash went by my head so fast I could hear it split the air. Big city streets, even in Florida, are not flat. At times, the car felt like it was attached to a roller coaster. I stopped looking when the speedometer passed 100 mph. And you know what? We were late for the game. But what a trip the ride was.

In West Palm, I was out with an officer whose radio called him to a domestic disturbance. Our destination was a series of row houses. Our car was resting in front of a stand of thick trees and shrubs. The configuration of the housing was a semi-circle. Three dirt roads were coming at us, and we would have no place to go. I suggested backup, but the deputy countered, "We don't even know what we have here." A woman in her late teens or early '20s had made the call and met us at the car. Her boyfriend had beaten her because their baby wouldn't stop crying. The boyfriend had taken off down one of the paths. He was a member of a notorious gang. She thought he would be back for gang-land punishment.

Now we had a problem. From any of those roads could come any number of gang members. My partner had to go into the house and then write a report. He said to me, "Stay with the car. Do you remember where the long gun safety is and how to disengage the gun?" I did. "You see anything at all, you grab that gun and yell for me." Now was the time for backup. It came. The gang members didn't. My blood pressure made my head feel like it was going to split. After my shift, I went drinking with the guys. Let's make it clear. I was a 50-year-old guy with no gun whose radio access was either in the car or, if heaven forbid, my partner got hurt, was attached to his shoulder. After it's over, it is the kind of experience that makes one wonder about the health of one's brain. Yet cops do it every day.

That's one of the real difficulties of being a cop. Often a taut situation can turn into nothing. Sometimes a tense situation turns into a car chase or chasing a K-9 through trees and brush pursuing a perp. The next call could be one requiring tenderness. The cop must learn how to go from being at high altitudes from adrenaline to coming back to earth and giving aid and comfort. It is so difficult to do that sometimes it doesn't happen. That's when we read about bad things in the newspaper.

Lastly, came a program that still gives me smiles, my appointment to restructure the chaplaincy. I found the chaplaincy recruiting process cumbersome. I needed a pipeline that would provide me with qualified chaplains. There were two ponds I could fish in. One was the MacArthur School at an Evangelical college, Palm Beach Atlantic University. The other was the Roman Catholic Regional Seminary. I constructed a curriculum that both schools accepted. Since I was teaching courses at both, I was a known quantity. The acceptances came quickly.

For reasons I'm not clear on, but for one, the Evangelical gambit didn't work. I knew because I was tipped off by two professors with whom I became friends. The students loved me. That caused jealousy among the ranks. More importantly, many of the professors felt strongly about a Jew teaching there. After a semester, it was over, although I did get one chaplain. He was a young man of great faith living with a forever illness that often made his life miserable. Issues like that tend to make great chaplains.

The Seminary program ran for five years until the certifying organization for the Seminary made having a Ph.D. a prerequisite for teaching. The course was an elective. The Seminary had a jam-packed curriculum. To add another class, you had to want it. Every year, we had a dozen or more candidates, some from other states and some from other countries. Aside from lectures, the candidates had to take notes as a deputy explained the workings of a patrol car. They also had to do a ride-a-long. Since the Seminary mandated some kind of chaplaincy experience, this one was easily approved.

What made this program so gratifying was my acceptance. I ate lunch with the seminarians and faculty. We organized a "cops against upperclassmen" annual softball game. There were easy before and after class discussions about their vocation, how they came to it, and what they hoped to do with it. Remember, these men were giving their lives to the priesthood, celibacy, and doing it at a time of tremendous and ongoing sexual scandal in the church. Yet, they were comfortable in their choice. I went to their graduations and when the Seminary built a new library, I asked my AJC members to donate Jewish books. So many books were donated that the Seminary library was able to establish a Jewish collection. I thought this very important because it would help the men understand the similarities and differences between Judaism and Catholicism. Again, I had an experience I couldn't have had in any other line of work.

"Writing isn't about making money, getting famous, getting dates, getting laid, or making friends. In the end, it's about enriching the lives of those who will read your work, and enriching your own life, as well. It's about getting up, getting well, and getting over. Getting happy, okay? Getting happy."

– Stephen King, on writing
A Memoir of the Craft

Book Six

Conclusion

There's a difference between an ending and the end.

"You can't wait for inspiration. You have to go after it with a club."

– Jack London

"I get a lot of letters from people. They say, "I want to be a writer. What should I do?" I tell them to stop writing to me and get on with it."

– Ruth Rendell

It is not easy to end a memoir. It doesn't mean I've run out of memories, which I haven't. It's a deeper sensation that asks how one makes it a conclusion and not an obituary.

To get to the end, we must go back to the beginning. That has a depressing similarity to life itself . . . This is the conclusion of the third and final book of the memoir, so this is the obit of the project I've been working on for four years. When I started, I decided that I could write these books in two styles. One would have the tinge of a Jewish neurotic standup comic (there's a bunch of redundancy in there . . .), the other could sound like tapes from a therapy session. I chose the former for two reasons.

First, I'm from Brooklyn in the '50s, where there was still a little dab of Woody Allen and a splash of Don Rickles in everybody. That style comes naturally to me. The second and more important reason is that I felt at the time I was writing these books, and I feared for a good time longer, the world needed a light, humorous, edgy book that was an easy read. Living in today's world is like being a dormouse. Once you push up the top of the teapot and look around, you want to drop back down into the darkness. I didn't want to thrust my readers into the darkness but give them a refuge with light. My reviewers have said I've succeeded, but that's a decision to be made only by each and every reader. I hope I've succeeded with you. **A five-star review on Amazon would be a welcome affirmation that I have.**

I should add that I've written each book as a stand-alone read. The first covers growing up from about 3-17. The second is about coming of age, about surviving in college on one's own. This one deals with the reality of life—work. I learned quickly that making work light and funny is hard. As the title says, "That's why they call it work." I tried my best to tickle your funny bone.

Remember my mentor telling me that half of what you learn in college is not learned in the classroom? He counseled me to go out of town, really out of state, if affordable, because the new geography, the new people, even the different foods were all learning experiences like grits or biscuits and gravy. So, it was with changing cities. I dated two girls, from different states, one a dyed-in-the-wool Southern Methodist and another a Mormon, both who tried to convert and marry me. That wouldn't have happened in Brooklyn. One learns from such things. Also, I saw a lot of the country because of work.

I also saw parts of the world. I was chosen as one of three representatives by the German government to spend three weeks traveling in Germany. The purpose was to show that democracy had taken hold and to see the ashes from which like the Phoenix had arisen. I went to my first of five concentration camps. When you see human ashes in ovens, it's hard to call it a learning experience. Yet, it surely is. I was personally subject to antisemitism in Poland. Another learning experience, this from people who were everyday folk. I visited Israel at least two dozen times. Israel is an encyclopedic learning experience.

Writing these books has been a "yea-boo" experience. I love writing. It's like composing music except with words. I loved taking trips up into what Woody Allen called "the attic of my mind." I found lots of things in piles, often having to move the ones on top to find the treasure troves beneath them. Exploring a vivid memory prompts remembering something else that has been tucked away, undisturbed, for decades.

Here's a learning experience. I was always curious to know why our extended family included everyone on my mom's side and no one on my dad's. One day I was giving a lecture in Delray Beach. At the end, a woman approached me and asked, "Does the name *Peshe* (Peter in Yiddish) mean anything to you?" I said yes, that was one of my father's uncles. She was his granddaughter. She invited me for tea. I popped the question: why don't I know anyone from my dad's side? Her answer? "Because your mother was a snob."

She explained that my mom's marriage to my dad, a dentist, was almost an arranged marriage. My grandma wanted her to marry a professional man and live a good life. My dad's uncles were all in the category of "tinkers, tailors, and candlestick makers." My mom wasn't going to step down the social and economic ladder now that she had stepped up. I went to elementary school with a cousin from my dad's side. His family lived no more than a long walk from us but in an apartment building, not a private house. His dad was a painter. I met my cousin's family once. End of story. Definite learning experience.

Then too, there was my job. I describe it as 33 years of going to graduate school. Much like my mentor said about what one learns in vs. out of the classroom, so it is with AJC. AJC is divided into two broad groups of workers. The "national staff" and the "field staff." The national staff were department heads and program specialists. They worked in the national office on 53rd Street and an almost national office in Washington, D.C. The D.C. office had staff that primarily dealt with the branches of the Federal Government.

The field staff, of which I was one, staffed the thirty-three offices in cities with significant Jewish populations across the country. There were also offices in France, Germany, and Israel. Besides ego, one main difference between the national and field staff was that the national staff members met with each other several times a week and sometimes several times a day. They developed friendships, lunch groups, discussed property investments and the ups and downs of their lives. Many, long retired, are still in touch. Geography made that very hard to happen between field staff members.

My first supervisor told me not to view my lay leaders as my friends. They would turn on me instantly as soon as they saw their wants in the agency not given to them. Remember my experience in Miami? That meant that unless a field director made friends outside of the chapter, the job could be lonely and full of phoniness as the director cultivated leaders and the leaders cultivated the director. While there were some semi-annual or, in some cases, quarterly meetings of field directors, they didn't produce the lasting relationships working at national did.

An example: I had a close friend, the director of the Cleveland Chapter. We had the same warped sense of humor and disdain for the national staff, many of whom radiated insufferability. He had a signature funny story about a particular type of chicken, the Rhode y Gralnick

Island Red. It became legendary. For a milestone in his life, I wrote to Frank Perdue, Jr., CEO of Perdue Chicken Farms for an autograph and requested a personal note. I got it, framed it, and he received it like the baby Jesus. The last time I heard from him was several years ago when he called to tell me he had just thrown it away. Nada since.

I had two supervisors with whom I felt I had a very close relationship. One I saw annually because his sister lives near me in Florida. One I saw once in New York for lunch and pocketbook shopping for my wife. The other I still trade emails with. Then there was another director. He was from Pittsburgh. We became friends. He came to me with tears in his eyes. He was in a difficult financial position. I lent him money. He paid it back. Have you heard from him in the last ten years? Me neither. *Asi es la vida* (such is life).

Yet the diversity in geography, the trips abroad, the visits to and from colleagues from other cities, no less the voluminous amount of reading materials on all manner of subjects from antisemitism to something called job-linked housing were a constant education. At one of my first meetings, I asked a different director in Pittsburgh, a ten-year veteran, how he coped with all the reading. In Atlanta, you will recall, I received the daily papers from each city in which I had a chapter to cover—Greensboro, Atlanta, Nashville, Memphis, and Birmingham (no digital editions then). I also had the same amount of reading he had. At times, it could be overwhelming. He said, "I sort them by subject and line the piles up around the floor. If I don't have to use a pile after ten days, I throw it away."

The next year he was fired, I think, for smoking pot in the office. I learned from that to either file everything, hide it before anyone from national came to visit, or throw it away immediately . . . and, of course, not to smoke pot in the office. Ba da bing.

I got to sit at the feet of giants and take in their wisdom. There was a "chat format" meeting between former Congressman and Nuremberg prosecutor, Morris Abram, and Norman Podhoretz, the founding editor of *Commentary Magazine*, a widely respected magazine with a small circulation. Its subscribers included diplomats, politicians, CEOs, and the leading academics of the day. Today it would be known as an influencer.

I had a study session of *Torah* with "Yitz" Greenberg, who was acknowledged amongst all branches of Judaism, as one of the great *Torah* scholars in America.

AJC had an Oral History Library. For many years, a staple at our annual meeting was an interview of one or more Jewish greats. We listened from the horse's mouth to the lives of Jewish stars, leaders of nations, great scientists, artists, and academics.

I listened to presidents, and I even introduced one, which was carried live around the world. There were Secretaries of State, U.S. Ambassadors and those from other countries, and FBI directors. And after a few years, the agency appointed me liaison to the Secret Service. That's a story worth telling. It didn't fit above because it isn't a chapter story, it's an annual meeting story. Here goes.

I was his designated greeter when Bush '43 spoke at our annual meeting. I had had the Secret Service liaison gig for several years, so I was comfortable. I also had things I could talk to him about while he was in the holding area behind the stage. My youngest son had played football and baseball with his nephews. I knew his brother Jeb, then Governor of Florida, well enough so that he recognized me on sight. 'turned out the "prez" is not much of a conversationist and didn't much care about my offerings.

George W. Bush, 43rd President of these United States. When we met, I didn't get this smile.

I was not supposed to introduce him, just introduce him to the guy who would introduce him. S!!t happens. The guy was late, and late is not something the Secret Service tolerates unless their boss has called the audible. Amongst details I'd learned, they had sealed all the manholes within about a mile of the

AMERICAN
JEWISH
COMMITTEE

89th Annual Dinner

May 4, 1995
Grand Hyatt Washington

Seating

A TIME OF CHANGE, A TIME OF CHALLENGE

venue and stopped the subway lines that emptied near it. That stuff had to be undone and quickly. Someone, I don't know who, saw the agent in charge signal, "Now!" Another agent shoved me in the back and through the curtain. Thank God, I grabbed at the mike. It kept me from doing a swan dive onto the front tables of the audience. Fortunately, I'd heard a lot of presidential introductions. I chose the one the Sergeant at Arms of the House of Representatives uses when the President is about to enter the chamber for the State of the Union. "Ladies and Gentlemen, it is a high honor and privilege . . ." I had enough presence of mind to remember his number and his name. As he entered, I exited, my body parts shaking like fall leaves in a breeze. That continued for about an hour.

Then there was this. One of the chapter directors had a member with mental issues. He thought he was a bird, except when he took his meds. This day he hadn't. I should preface this with his attire. Black pants, black shirt, and sunglasses so dark his eyes weren't visible. Now picture this. At the podium is the director of the FBI. Every sight angle towards him had one or more armed FBI agents. All their eyes looked like in another life they had belonged to a hawk. The birdman took flight.

Sometimes, as the saying goes, "Better lucky than good." I had just taken Red Cross training on how to handle such situations. I got up as he lifted from the table, stretched out his arms, and began lazily to soar around the dining room. Talking softly and gently, I approached him. At each of his turns, I remained in front of him. I told one of the agents, "I got this." I managed to keep half a ballroom's distance between him and the podium until the bird's chapter director realized what was happening. She hailed a doctor who had the meds. All's well that ends well.

Here's another "kid from Brooklyn meets a president" story. First-term president Bill Clinton spoke to one of the conventions. When the ballroom opened, I noticed a couple who looked like they had come out of a Norman Rockwell painting. They strolled in and took seats at the first-row center table. He was absorbed in focusing his camera (no cell phone cameras), pulling things out and putting things into his camera bag, leaning this way, standing a foot or so that way, doing everything that would give him a perfect shot. All the motions made a Secret Service agent very jittery.

The ballroom filled, and Mr. Middle America stood on his chair, preparing for the President's entrance. Nobody in town would have a picture like this! The agent in charge came over to me and said curtly, "get him off that chair." So, I did. Politely, I said that this was not permissible, but his drive to have the photo that would be talked about at barbecues and card games for years to come was not to be derailed. Minutes later he popped up, reaching in and out of the bag, again with the focusing and changing lens, again with finding the best angle, and again with the agent who this time said to me, "Make that stop, or I'll have to handle it." I sat him down, and don't you know, minutes later up he popped. This time I moved before the agent did. I walked over to him, helped him from the chair, and said, "Sir, turn around a minute. See that guy with the button on his collar and the thing in his ear?" I got a nod of assent. "Well," I continued, "He said to tell you that if you got up on that chair again, he would have to shoot you." He had said, of course, no such thing. But hey, improv is the most skilled form of acting, and that's what I was doing. That was the end of the incident, but not of the story.

I was part of the team making sure the crowd didn't push too close to the stage. Clinton, a Southerner, and great politician stood, and waved, called out hellos, and subsequently was the last to leave. He walked right by me. I had the meeting program in my hand, and I thrust it out begging . . . "Mr. President, could I trouble you for an autograph?" At that moment, one of his staffers pushed me aside and said, "The president has no time for this" and with other staffers shoved him towards the exit. I was both crest-fallen and a bit peeved. About two minutes later a person more crestfallen than I came towards me. It was "Mr. Hurry Along" staffer. He said, "The president would like to know your name and asked that I get the program you had." I did. He raced out to the motorcade and then, panting, raced back to me, with a presidential autograph, which hangs, framed, over my right shoulder as I write this. And for you historians, I do know that Clinton came before Bush. He just came out of my memory after him . . .

These are stories one just can't make up. Well, I guess I could have, but I didn't.

And so, now we come to the end of it.

Or so I thought. Then I discussed the manuscript with my publisher. He said I was missing the current piece of my life and had much more to write. Writing, he reminded me, is work. Hard work. So let me bring you up to date.

I opened with the "why" of my writing. The what and how are missing. Together the what and how are what makes writing work. I wrote two books before this trilogy. They were not my idea. My wife and my editor at the Boca Raton News said there was a book in the 900 plus columns I'd written up to that time. 'turns out there were two. I, however, had to figure out how to make them work as a book. Then it hit me.

The columns, it struck me, were still relevant. Things I had written about 10, 15, and even 20 years ago were still on the front pages. If I grouped them into subject categories, adding an introduction to each section and adding the current event relationship, maybe I would have something. To have something, you must call it something.

I came up with three titles, all of which my editor said stank. He pointed out that there was humor, sometimes sharp, sometimes sardonic, and what he felt was an unusual twist on approaching the topics. He wanted a title that would give the prospective reader a hint of that. The winning choice? "Mirth, Wind, and Ire."

Now I had a title. It would be a gross understatement to say I had no idea what came next or how to do it. My editor told me that I had to put the book together first. That I did. Then I found a typist. She created a manuscript that my editor went to town on. It took a few months, but I now had a book.

Lots of people write books for themselves or their families. I had no interest in doing that. Some people are so hell-bent on seeing their work in print that they fall prey to what are called Vanity Press publishers. These people charge an arm and a leg to print the book. They then disappear. The one virtue is that the process is easy, except for writing the check. Reading up on "next steps," I realized I now needed an agent.

I bought a copy of one of the industry's bibles, *The Writer's Market*. It has contact information lists for agents and publishers—what they are and are not interested in. This process is like applying to college. You need thick skin to deal with all the rejection letters. The book warns you that some agents are so busy they won't respond. I got nowhere, and I didn't get there fast.

Then I got turned on to the self-publishing end of the industry. We came up with a neat graphic and were off to the races. I sold about 100 of them. I also had hundreds and hundreds of columns left over. My editor said, "So do it again." I did. The title I came up with was just short of brilliant: "More Mirth, Wind, and Ire." Ba da boom. The full title is Mirth, Wind, and Ire: Essays on the Contemporary Political and Social Scene—With a Little Humor Thrown In." If you are interested in the intractability of this nation's social and political issues, you can still reach into cyberspace and order copies. http://smashwords.com/books/view/758411 and 692523.

Then came the trilogy, which did not start as a trilogy. My whole life, I've observed the world around me. I come from Brooklyn, as you've read a head-spinning number of times by now. People from Brooklyn see the world differently than the rest see it, even differently than the rest of their fellow New Yorkers. Aside from Barbra Streisand, Brooklyn is known for its comedians. Most Brooklynites think they are comedians and but for lousy luck, would have been Woody Allen, Don Rickles, or Buddy Hackett. Put me in with that lot.

Having a very retentive mind for things that most people wouldn't notice or remember, would hear, and forget, I had as many stories as Milton Berle had jokes ("I got a million of 'em, folks!" he would say.). Each happening became a story, some of which I'd written after college, others during downtime at various jobs. I again needed a title. I had one. My wife's reaction was, "You can't put that into print!" My editor said, "No one will buy a book with that title." I stuck to my guns. I thought that the title on the spine of a book or reaching out from a computer screen would be a grabber. Besides, anyone from Brooklyn and several surrounding states would get it immediately, so I insisted on *The War of the Itchy Balls and Other Notes from Brooklyn*. This time I had a publisher. He changed Notes to Tales, and we were set to go. Or not.

In the years between "Mirth . . ." and Brooklyn, the publishing industry had dramatically changed. Only the major houses that paid tremendous advances to people who were household names did marketing. They had to ensure that they protected their investment. Smaller publishers did editing and publishing and usually nothing more. Marketing has now become the author's job, but we're not at that job yet.

Since I drew blanks on getting representation and noted another change in the industry, a door opened. The difference was the growth of what are called hybrid publishers. These publishers share the costs with the author, provide press releases, provide marketing tips, send out notices nationally and internationally to Amazon, Barnes and Noble, and international distributors, do bookkeeping, and send and keep track of royalties.

Just like with seeking agents, the author has to learn how to write a query letter and a book proposal. Learning these requires going online and reading reams of information to find the style that suits the writer. These go to agents. It's like applying to college. I came up with three who were interested. One had two strong points the others didn't. One, he was in Florida, and we could meet personally. The other was he was a New York Jew. I felt that for this book, I would need someone who had lived its iconic culture, language, and humor.

Now there was more work to do. Books have endorsements, a person, or persons, hopefully of some note, who would say something nice about the book to be printed on its cover. Who would they be for me? Brainstorm! My brother had recently died. A who's who of the broadcast news industry populated his memorial service.

I shared the speaking honors with Brian Williams, whom my brother had been tasked to prepare to take over Tom Brokaw's position. Also, Lynn Sher was in the audience and someone who was very solicitous of me during the service. I asked them both, and Holy Broadcast Booth, Bat readers, they both said yes. Sher, it turned out, is a memoirist and was more than happy to encourage me.

A note about Brian. He is a natural comic, quick of wit with perfect timing. I could understand the rumors that he was angling for Jay Leno's job. To follow him onto the stage takes moxie. I was quickly set with two well-known endorsers. Williams even asked me if I liked what he wrote and if not should he change anything? Once you catch a bird, you don't let it go to see if you can catch it again. "Perfect!" I replied.

I remember one self-effacing story he told. My brother, as executive producer, was in the production booth every night. He'd watch a reporter's story. Often if it were good, he'd call and tell the person, "Good job!" and point out why. Everything was a teaching moment. If it was not good . . . still a teaching moment.

Williams was in the field doing a top-of-the-news story. He did it well. What was my brother's teaching moment? "Brian, now that you're going to be making a fortune, for God's sake, go out and buy some good clothing. Get gone the "in the bush" look ." For those of you who were Williams' fans, you know he became the fashion plate of the industry.

For the GW book endorsers, I had a problem. I'd run out of big names but not out of ideas. Florida Atlantic University had awarded me an honorary Doctor of Human Letters degree. What about the now-retired president? I asked. He said yes. I had a relationship with the president of my alma mater, George Washington University, when our daughter was there. We spoke on the phone; I sent him a few chapters. I got his endorsement. Two university presidents for a book about a university? Not bad. I wanted one more. At this time, the former mayor of Boca Raton, who I knew quite well, was the head of the regional transportation system in the tri-county area. I got his endorsement and didn't think it would serve me until I read what he wrote. It was a one-word winner—"Hysterical!" he wrote.

So, that was it for endorsers. Now came the pictures. My publisher felt strongly that a book of words was boring. Pictures kept the reader tuned in. We split the task. I went through family albums; he went onto the net. It didn't take long to have 40 or so pictures linked to the stories in the book. I even found one of an itchy ball. Now we come to the next hurdle. It's called copyright law.

We think what's on the internet is there for the taking. Much is not. They are protected by the "owner" having a copyright on the text or picture. That means they own it, and the user must request permission to use it and/or pay for using it. For a low budget author that can add up. There are many services that have bought the copyrights on millions of things. The author can use one of these services or . . . you learn there is something in the law called the public domain. In a writer's case, that means there is free access to an unbelievable number of pictures. One can use segments of a song, a line or maybe a paragraph. The copywrite expires after a certain number of years and those things are then free for the taking.

Quotes can be an excellent tool to punch up a point that is being made or illustrate it. Unless the sayer's foundation or trust owns them, they, too, are floating balloons to be grabbed by the needy. I use the public domain site often, at least weekly for my blog (http://atleastfrommyperspectiveblog.wordpress.com). For the struggling artist, it is a Godsend. A good "indie"—independent publisher—helps one use these tools to make, in my case, a much better product than I alone was able to produce.

The book has been read (mind you, not yet edited), been put in proper order, had pictures and quotes added (in my Brooklyn book, my publisher found dozens of quotes from famous and not-so-famous Brooklynites). Now it is ready to be edited . . . and edited . . .

and reedited . . . Both *The War of the Itchy Balls* . . . and *George Washington Never Slept Here* ran this gauntlet five times. Stephen King suggests that some authors do this themselves once or twice, eliminating every extraneous word and thought before giving it to the editor. He cautions that removing one's own hard work to give birth to a book makes the writer feel like children are being murdered. You must write to understand that.

So, we're done. Or so you'd think. You'd be wrong. All these words, pictures, and quotes must fit on the same size piece of paper. Making that happen is the printer's job. The publisher, author, and printer also collaborate on the book's front and back cover. Most books today are paperbacks because the costs of a hardcover book are breathtaking. The printer then runs several copies, and one gets to read it yet again. But hold on there, cowboy, we're not out of the corral yet.

The publisher has to do some technical stuff. One of the most important ones is getting a Library of Congress number and filing for a copyright. Without a copyright, one's words can become anyone's words in terms of usage. Now we come to another one of the most significant changes in the publishing industry. It is known as POD, print on demand. If I'm Michele Obama and my book is being published hard and soft-cover and being hyped all over the country and the world, and is being breathlessly awaited by books stores, an advance run of thousands of copies is done. You walk into your local bookstore and there is the book. I was just in Barnes and Noble, and two faces commanded the center space. One was Mrs. Obama's, the other Prince Harry's. One that was not there was mine.

Here is where the author becomes a businessperson. The publisher has a deal with the printer so the author can buy his/her work at a discount. Authors are urged to do speaking engagements at social clubs, service clubs, programs at houses of worship, stand on a milk crate and read to the world (just kidding on that one) and have a supply of books to sell. The publisher also submits the book to Barnes & Noble and Amazon. These two are where the largest number of sales take place.

One must learn about Facebook and Google ads. Another potential help is a micro-marketing operation called Nextdoor. It enables one to target marketing by zip code. Facebook also has groups. You can advertise to those groups. I belong to three different Brooklyn-oriented groups, which I alerted to the arrival of my prize. Nor should you be thin-skinned and not be a huckster to your friends, family, and any other lists you have. I have 3,700 Facebook friends. They are not my nearest and dearest, but they'll all hear from me.

Three months later, your first royalty check arrives. It is a genuine thrill—until you look at the amount and realize giving up your day job is out of the question. But then again, you are now a published author.

There's a fundamental difference between an editor of columns and an editor of books. A book editor employs up to three different kinds of editing. Not to worry. I won't bore you. If you're fascinated, google editing. My publisher gave the manuscript to his editor. There were five back and forths. I read the manuscript of close to 80,000 words five complete times. It is said that when a writer has gotten to the point that he hates reading his manuscript, then he's ready to have it published. I was more than more than ready.

Someone told me she loved reading it, how funny it was. I said, "it's a lot funnier now than it was both living it and writing it . . .

I hope you enjoyed reading it as much as I did living it.

"Most people work just hard enough not to get fired and get paid just enough money not to quit."

– George Carlin, Stand-up
Comedian and Author

"My keyboard must be broken, I keep hitting the escape key, but I'm still at work."

– Unknown Author

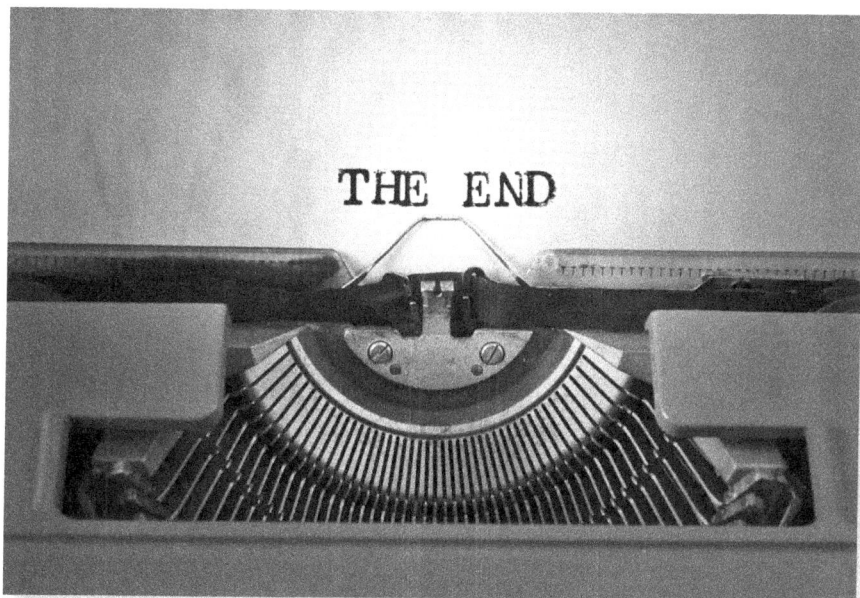

That's All He Wrote, Folks.

www.ingramcontent.com/pod-product-compliance
Lightning Source LLC
Chambersburg PA
CBHW070348090426
42733CB00009B/1328